FIVE
Challenges
for the Once and
Future Church

Loren B. Mead

An Alban Institute Publication

The Publications Program of The Alban Institute is assisted by a grant from Trinity Church, New York City.

Copyright © 1996 by The Alban Institute, Inc. All rights reserved.

This material may not be photocopied or reproduced in any way without written permission.

Library of Congress Catalog Card #96-85718
ISBN 1-56699-175-7

To
The members and staff of St. Alban's Parish —
ministers, every one of them

and especially to
the Tuesday morning eucharist group

CONTENTS

INTRODUCTION

I wonder if we have the time.

Do we who love our religious traditions and systems have the time to redesign, reinvent, or redevelop them for the next generation? Can we, who have inherited such riches from earlier generations of faithful people, pass on an even stronger heritage of faith to the next generations?

These are the kinds of questions that have led me to write this book. Let me be specific. As I look at the future of the church, I see extraordinary challenges lying ahead of us. I honestly do not know if we—as a set of institutions—can survive the difficulties we face.

I often feel very lonely in this concern. I find many of my colleagues going on as they always have. I see people and institutions making plans for tomorrow as if it will be a replica of yesterday. Where I do see energy for facing difficulties, I find little sense of urgency. I get the sense that people hope it will all go away if we just keep our heads down and keep putting one foot ahead of the other. Where I sense energy for change, I too often sense an inadequate understanding of the depth of the issues we face; maybe a few minor adjustments will put things back on track.

I get angry when I hear those who tell us that all we need to do is turn back the clock to a time they remember as more peaceful, settled days for the church. I remember the times they talk about, and they were not better times; they preserved many kinds of injustices and inequities.

Several dimensions of the life of the church make me wonder whether or not we have time. Here's what I see.

First, those with the most at stake in preserving the status quo are the ones who have most of the power to change our systems.

Second, our leaders have short tenure in leadership roles. Most of the changes needed require facing critical controversies. Most leaders in our society—secular and religious—seem to want to leave the hard issues for the next generation. It is the Marie Antoinette version of leadership. Remember that the deluge did not wait until after Marie Antoinette! She lost her head. I am clear that the changes ahead will be hard to carry out. We have no chance if we do not have leaders who can look further down the road and make hard choices for the future.

Third, I see a progressive erosion of the financial resources that have supported our institutions. With a short-term approach that hopes only to balance the current budget and has no care for the future. Almost no attention is being paid to the financial crises that are ten or twenty years in the future.

Fourth, I note an increasing lack of trust among the people, the agencies, and the institutions that make up our denominational systems. Our religious institutions follow the lead of our political institutions in having lost any sense of patience or civility with one another. Each person or group seems to be in competition with all others—for scarce resources, for supremacy of one point of view, sometimes for vindication or pure revenge for past losses.

John Kotter of the Harvard Business School has worked with many institutions attempting to be more successful in a changing environment. Although the church is not exactly the same as other organizations,[1] several of Kotter's impediments to organizational transformation fit our challenge in the churches.[2]

Not establishing a great enough sense of urgency. Within my experience churches are denying the reality of the threat around us. As long as church leaders—pastors, bishops, executives, theologians— continue to talk about "bottoming out" and cover up disastrous truths with language about "really exciting missionary opportunities in spite of unexpected reversals," we continue to infantalize the laity of the churches, assuming that they are too weak to take straight talk. What about the denomination that promised to open several hundred new churches but ran out of money in the first six months? What about the denomination that expects to have to close a thousand churches in the next decade? Who is talking straight to members about these things? And if the truth is soft-pedaled, who can be surprised that there is little urgency about the need for transformation?

Lacking a vision. You have a hard time nowadays finding a self-respecting church organization or institution without an engraved vision statement. Problem is, it's hard to distinguish one from any other. And most of them confuse a vision with a dream or with public relations. The dreams tend to be all-inclusive, having global scope and just a bit of triumphalism. The public relations visions represent what feels like a "positioning" of the church's image in terms of appealing to a particular market. Many of the visions give evidence of hard work over time by hundreds of people who have engaged in data gathering, assessing feedback, and all the other processes we consultants can think up. But what comes out at the other end rarely seems to express the passions of a people.

I know of one exception, one that rang so true to me that I still remember it two years after I first heard it. It is the vision the Church of the Brethren articulated to say who and what they are and what they want to be:

Continuing the work of Jesus.
Peacefully.
Simply.
Together.

As is the case with other vision statements, a lot of time and hard work went into the construction of this profoundly simple declaration. But what separates it from the others is that it rings especially true. It is not ostentatious. It makes no unreasonable claims. It toots no horns. It expresses something between a reality and a hope and is clearly built upon the traditions of that family of the church. No one but the Brethren could have said that. I am sure the Church of the Brethren is facing just as difficult a period of transformation as any of the other families of faith, but I think this vision will give them a touchstone for their transformation.

The real power of a vision is that it can put you in touch with who and what you truly are, even as you articulate that which you intend to be. Without a clear vision, Kotter warns, transformation is difficult. What I would add to his warning is my experience that visions are gifts. They represent an intuitive leap from one's historic identity into the future.[3] There is more listening than talking in discerning visions. Discerning visions depends more on waiting on the Lord than on sending out questionnaires.

Declaring victory too soon. Kotter suggests this third warning churches need to heed. It may be that churches are just too impatient. After the first effort, even before the effort is evaluated, a victory is celebrated. Indeed, all too often I have found churches celebrate as a victory an idea that has just been invented, even before it is tried out. In my experience this is caused by the necessity to garner lots of energy to try something out. So the new thing is trumpeted as the solution to all the problems facing the church—even before it is tested. Church people want to fix things. The problem? I don't see anything facing the church that is likely to be fixed in our lifetimes, if then. Some things may never be fixed. Yet if we do not sell our approach as a way to fix what's wrong, we are not likely to get a chance to try it out.[4]

Do we, then, have time? Is the crisis such that we face an inevitable collapse of the familiar and comforting supports that our religious congregations have provided in the past?

I honestly do not know. Assuming the best—that we do have time— I have tried to identify five key obstacles we face if we would leave a church for future generations that is stronger than the one we have been given. These obstacles are not sequential. We face all of them all at once. Some will press upon us more powerfully than others. Some of us will be seized by one or two of the obstacles, and we may spend our whole lives struggling with them.

Two things encourage me. First, the churches have a tradition of laypeople and clergy who rise to challenges. Second, the churches have solid grounds for facing hard things.

Time and time again in its history, the church has come to what seemed to be a dead end. From the early controversies between Hellenistic and Judaistic leaders to the crises of the reformation, the church has discovered that God somehow raises up the new people, the new ideas, the new energy with which to address whatever it is that comes down the road. I see all about me today church leaders with incredible commitment to the future of the church, often with little support from those in the structures. I honor the faith of Catholic women who build for a new church in spite of opposition. I am uplifted by the laymen and women of hundreds of congregations who keep on keeping on in the face of clergy indifference to their concerns. I am humbled by the sacrifices I know some clergy make to try to do their work in a new way. I am inspired as I see bishops and executives taking their careers in their hands to open doors for change. Many of those people—clergy and lay—pay a considerable price for standing against the status quo, but they stand in a long tradition of such leaders. I trust in God that more leaders will come.

I am also encouraged because our religious tradition is not grounded on winning. Time and time again, we discover that it is in weakness we are made strong, in foolishness we are led to wisdom. This understanding is the cornerstone of who we are. We know that darkness comes before the dawn, not as some sentimental saying, but because that is how it has been in our encounter with God. When we as churches worry about whether or not we will "make it," we give in to the success-oriented philosophies of this world. We know that God's presence is with us through the valley of the shadow of death, yes, but we also know that that presence goes beyond death.

In this book I discuss the obstacles we need to address in building the church of the future. I do so with humility; I expect to be proven wrong many, many times. But I do so also with considerable confidence in what lies ahead.

In the final analysis, the outcome is in the hands of God. For now, here are the five challenges I see we have ahead of us:

To transfer the ownership of the church.
To discover new structures for the church.
To discover a passionate spirituality.
To make the church a new community and source of community.
To become an apostolic people.

CHAPTER 1

CHALLENGE 1:
To Transfer the Ownership of the Church

In America the church is owned by its clergy.

That is what *clericalism* means.

I don't know of any church that would formally agree with my opening statement. That is why I have stated it so baldly; I want us to think about what we do, not what we say we do.

As with any "ism"—sexism, racism, ageism—clericalism is not about what we say we believe. It is not about how we want to believe. It is about what we do. An "ism" is not about particular actions or conscious intentions. It is about a pattern of action, a stance of life that is under the control of larger systems of power that run counter, often, to what the individual genuinely believes he or she intends. This is why good-hearted, well-intentioned people can vote for a measure that will damage the rights of African Americans or Hispanic Americans and then say, "But I'm not a racist." Similarly, few clergy or laypeople would claim to approve of a system of clericalism that maintains clergy as a privileged caste. "Isms" are about people—both perpetrators and victims of discriminations—getting trapped by the power systems around them.[1]

Clericalism is an all-embracing assumption that shapes how we think about churches and how we think about the roles each of us plays in the life of the church. It is about how we expect each other to act—a powerful expectation that we rarely talk about. Clericalism, for us in the churches, is like the water in which a fish swims. To the fish the water is invisible, its existence unacknowledged, but it constitutes the world in which the fish lives; it limits what the fish can do and be.

I'd like to tell a story to make my point clear. Even if we cannot see the water we swim in, we may get some hunches about what clericalism is and how it sneaks up on us.

A Simple Fable

Once upon a time in a kingdom far away there was a wide valley between two high mountain ranges. The valley had rich farm land and abounded in game. The river supplied an ample variety of fish. The lavish valley tempted vagabonds. Almost every spring the farmers and householders faced armed groups intending to steal from the fields, carrying home livestock and sometimes even children. The king lived a long ways away, on the other side of the mountains. Hearing of the troubled times, he asked a trusted ally to oversee the valley—to restore the peace and prosperity.

The new lord of the valley drew on the practices and skills he had learned and then perfected defending the people of other valleys. Many thought they were ancient skills, first used by Arthur in the days of Camelot. He established orders of knights and squires skilled in martial arts, and he called on them to protect the valley from outsiders. In battle after battle he led them to victory. Gradually peace returned to the valley.

In the peaceful reign, the knights and squires came regularly to the lord's castle to practice their arts; while maintaining their leadership, they taught younger candidates the intricacies of the skills and customs. As the knights aged, they inducted the younger trainees into responsible positions. All over the kingdom stories were told of the valley between the mountains and how peace had returned to it through the strength of the lord and his knights and squires.

It wasn't long before the farms flourished, with harvests richer far than ever before. The serfs and freemen were able to till the soil without fear. They nurtured the fields and tended the crops. In time they were able to build the trading ships to carry produce down the river to distant ports. Every year the valley became more secure and stronger. The taxes the lord required for the upkeep of the castle and the knights and squires seemed inconsequential. It was a fair exchange for the peace and security the people found.

In time the external threats disappeared, and the memories of pillage became remote. As that happened, new questions arose. Was there really a need for a new wing on the castle? Did all the knights need new swords every other year? Were the costs of the lord's stable getting out of hand? Do we really need as many knights in training this year? Was it necessary for people of the valley to send finances and even some troops to help the far-off king fighting battles in other valleys? Couldn't taxes be trimmed?

The heart of the valley's prosperity was the productivity of the farmers, but the decisions about the life of the valley were left in the hands of the lord and his knights who held conferences and retreats from time to time to rethink how their skills could be improved or the castle made stronger. At great conferences in the castle, the lord called upon his knights for advice and counsel.

Granted, great care was taken to see that the valley was secure against any and all possible enemies, but the farmers and other citizens eventually grew restless. The praise for the lord turned to complaint.

The lord spoke to his knights: "I hear the valley people are restless. You know, as I do, that we ordered our life here to preserve the peace of the land. We have made many sacrifices to bring security and peace to the valley. We must have strong knights and squires and an impregnable castle. So long as we keep these strong, the valley will be peaceful and the farms prosperous." Although the knights agreed to a man, the unrest spread. People in the valley continued to ask why so many knights were necessary and whether their upkeep needed to be so expensive. They made suggestions about how costs might be reduced.

The lord of the valley reassured the people: "We who have been trained in the skills of diplomacy and warfare know more about the threats to our peace than you can know. You must understand that the society we have formed is the one that best protects your prosperity."

Over time, the lord discovered two ways of dealing with farmers who insisted on verbalizing their complaints. The most reliable method was to recognize the questioning as a sign of potential leadership. The most difficult questions reflected really thoughtful analyses of what was going on. Farmers asking such questions (there were not too many of them) were invited to become special trainees in knight school. They studied diplomacy and philosophy; they learned to wield the weapons of the knights and were given swords. Upon graduation, they were invited to sit as squires first; if they did well, finally they were knighted. They sat in the councils of the lord of the valley. Interestingly enough, their questions about the rights and wrongs of the exercise of power tended to disappear. They came to discover that the way the knights thought was right after all. And, yes, the language of debate and discussion nurtured in their training did seem more useful than the language of the farmers.

The farmers were pleased to see some of their own "making it" among the knights. They cheered lustily for the ex-farmer knights in the annual castle tournaments.

The lord used another, quite different, approach with other articulate critics. If one was particularly impassioned, the lord would invite that critic to address council meetings, giving special honor, asking the critic to repeat the most appalling things about the inequities of the system. Council members listened carefully, asked penetrating questions, and took notes. They then sent the critics home with strong applause and statements of genuine gratitude. The critics earned a kind of fame as critics. Their farmer colleagues were proud of them and their outspokenness, "telling it like it is" even to the powers that be. Those who spoke their criticisms most forcefully were celebrated and even sent by the lord to speak in other valleys where both they and their lord became known for their challenging approach to change. Some of these critics were even invited to the king's court to there give witness to their convictions.

But not much changed.2

Lessons of the Fable

This fairy tale connects us to the issue of ownership. In the story the lord and the knights formed a power group that made the rules for the good of the community, a concept in which they genuinely believed, having used it as the basis for rescuing the valley from chaos and returning it to safety and prosperity. Similarly, "for the good of the community," they created the rules that, at least in the beginning, were needed for an orderly society. But the rules did not change as the situation changed. And over time, those who benefitted most from the rules were least likely to advocate change. Yes, the knights and the lord believed the rules to be right, but they also were accustomed to them and knew how to enforce them.

If, by chance, it were also true that the knights and squires loved all the pageantry, the tournaments, and the castle life—and if they were not fully aware that their decisions just happened to support their own privileges—who could deny them those small things?

And the lord's strategies for dealing with dissent are pretty transparently the strategies evident in clericalism as I have experienced it: In the church the articulate, challenging lay leader is either encouraged to go off to seminary—to understand the rules and learn the language—or informally ordained as the church's "pet prophet," riding the lecture circuit from judicatory to judicatory to the crowds' applause. And so we see evidence of the lord's two methods for handling dissenters: either co-opt them into the power system or encapsulate and "sponsor" their activities outside the power system, thereby diluting their effectiveness.

This fable illustrates, albeit obliquely, the institutional ways in which the ecclesiastical power system inhibits the churches' ability to respond to the needs of the current and future age.

Evidence of Clericalism

What characteristics of clericalism indicate the present ownership of the churches?

1. Churches Spend Their Money on Clergy

Almost all the professional salaries paid by churches are paid to clergy. Most laypeople who work for the institutional church receive nonprofessional salaries and work at the lower, nonpolicy-making levels of the institution. After World War II several denominations with a strong history of giving lay pastors full responsibility for a congregation moved rapidly to replace those lay leaders with seminary-educated, ordained clergy. Although some denominations now face an oversupply of clergy, those denominations continue to worry about employing clergy. I see no similar organized concern for unemployed laity.

Probably, and without meaning to do so, the churches have encouraged clergy to feel that a church job is an entitlement. A lay friend once expressed it caustically: "Sometimes it looks to me as if the church is just an employment agency for clergy!"

Clergy receive the lion's share of all the laity's contributions to their churches. In many cases the churches get a bargain—because of the outstanding quality of the clergy. But the fact remains that this is where the money goes. And we do not say so very clearly. Three investigators, trying to discover how many dollars clergy actually "cost" the average congregation, unearthed another side of the problem: Churches report the actual amounts spent on clergy in such convoluted ways that it's almost impossible for an outsider to compare what one clergyperson costs as compared with another, even within the same denomination.[3]

2. Decisions Are Made Primarily by the Clergy

Most decisions in churches are made primarily by clergy even though they have a high personal stake in many of those decisions, especially about the use of money. Minimum salary scales are voted in church meetings that clergy are paid to attend. Laypeople are not paid to attend such meetings. Over time decisions increasingly reflect the thinking of the clergy. Thus, the decision-making process becomes responsive to the self-interest of the clergy. (The knights truly believe that knightly leadership is in the best interest of all the people of the valley; knights do not seem to realize that they may be influenced by what is best for them more than by what is best for the farmers.)

Clergy often cite recent patterns (in the last three or four decades) of rotating congregational lay leadership to point to the strength and breadth of lay ownership of decision making. In fact this pattern has had quite the opposite effect. Rotating lay leadership has actually increased clergy power and ownership in most congregations. When lay leadership rotates every three or four years, the lay leaders are "evicted" just about the time they learn the ropes. I do not have a good alternative to offer, but I do point out that rotating leadership among a large group of laypeople effectually eliminates the strength and ownership of the lay voice.

3. Standards Are Determined by the Clergy

Denominational books of order and canons reflect clergy power in decision making. Specifically, most denominations have written into their rule books a definition of a "first-class" congregation that generally includes leadership by a full-time clergyperson serving at a denominationally determined minimum salary. This is more than a rule-book statement: By dint of long practice, this has become a self-evident standard.[4] Congregations unable to afford clergy understand themselves to be "second class." The standard norm is reinforced in that a congregation's becoming "fully self-supporting" (on the basis of these financial indicators) is cause for judicatory-wide celebration. Congregations that can no longer maintain the standard are seen to have "fallen behind," failed in a substantial way. Their "failure" is deplored by the judicatory staff and boards, and such congregations are given less voice in judicatory meetings. The standards of effective ministry are defined primarily in terms of the congregation's ability to employ a full-time clergyperson. This leads to the corollary standard that a congregation is somehow deficient if it does not have a resident clergyperson. A congregation even temporarily without a full-time pastor is considered "at risk" and becomes a worry for the judicatory executive or bishop. Such congregations are often described as being vacant. Bishops have told me that they have to hurry to get a pastor installed because otherwise "it will all go to pot." The standard is clear and, self-enforcing, in spite of any demonstrable proof that many congregations do well even during extended periods without ordained clergy leaders.

4. Denominational Decision Making, Skewed to Smaller Congregations, Emphasizes Clergy Voices

Within denominational decision-making processes, power often remains predominately in rural, small congregations, with larger congregations disproportionately underrepresented. The standards of the books of order and canons (set by generations of clergy-dominated meetings) affirm that "true" congregations must have a full-time pastor who, as such, is expected to attend the decision-making, policy-setting meetings of the judicatory. This is one more reason why every congregation, no matter how small, works sacrificially to find a way to support a pastor. And those pastors, representing the concerns of their small congregations, overrepresent the rural population when compared to the number of clergy representing the larger congregations which have fewer clergy per capita. This results in underrepresentation of large-congregation laity *and* underrepresentation of large-congregation clergy.

Of course this reality varies according to the denominational polity, but the weighting occurs in practice even when the written rules contradict that intention. Early in the nineteenth century, representation in Britain's House of Parliament was found to have followed a similar

pattern, with rural areas having become vastly overrepresented in proportion to the population of the growing cities. "[Rotten] boroughs" had full
representation, while urban areas had virtually none. Significant issues
arose because of the gulf between the rural and urban needs. Dramatic
political changes resulted in redrawing constituency lines, and the predominately rural House of Lords was stripped of its power. The change
was significant enough that it was called revolution. Such redress has not
happened in the churches.

5. The Clergy, Not the Laity, Is Trained in the Language of the Institution

Debate about what is and is not important to the institutional church is
often couched in language of historic controversies and issues; the language of academic theology is the approved medium of conversation.
Few laypeople have been educated in the language and history of the
controversies, so they enter the debate significantly handicapped.[5] Clergy
insist that important issues be given "rigorous theological reflection,"
often without defining what that means. Laity are asked to play that
game if their ideas are to be taken seriously. In my experience working
with clergy and executives making important decisions, I cannot remember ever actually having "rigorous theological reflection" brought into
the decision making. The decisions seemed to be made with the same
view of pragmatism, hope, and values that was used in nonclergy decisions.[6] The term, however, is used to invalidate nonclergy input to the
conversation. It reinforces the power of the clergy in making important
decisions.

6. Education for Clergy Is a Major Financial Investment

All of the major denominations invest heavily in the training and education of clergy. They invest modestly, if at all, in the education of the
laity. This disparity is dramatic in the churches' very large investment in
institutions of theological education. I see no institution of lay education
in any denomination that represents the kind of spending of the most
modest seminary. Seminaries of some denominations have far more

endowment than the entire denomination. The long-term investments earmarked for future education of clergy suggest that the policy of focusing resources on the clergy is being set for generations to come. Per capita education costs for clergy have escalated as have other costs in higher education. Costs per year of pastoral service have multiplied much more rapidly as older seminary students look forward to shorter and shorter periods of professional service.

7. The Clergy Controls "How One Changes the Rules"

A friend moving from one profession to another once told me, "I've decided to go to law school because lawyers write all the rules. They even write the rules about how you change the rules."

In the institutional church, the same could be said about the clergy. To facilitate institutional change one must be prepared to contend with the clergy—the group with the strongest voice in church councils and deep-rooted knowledge of institutional language.

My colleagues who consult with congregations acknowledge one rule of thumb: Clergy cannot make change happen by themselves, but they almost always have veto power.

The power of the clergy—I have described it even as ownership—is far-reaching. Over the generations the voice of the clergy has built and sustained many of the familiar and useful structures of religious life. This is true in all denominations, not just those seen as hierarchical. In some cases that power is located more locally; in others the power resides in clerical hierarchies. Several things need to be said about this power system.

The Issues

Conflict of Interest

We need to recognize that a classic conflict of interest is at work here. Clergy-dominated institutions make many decisions in which clergy have a direct stake: salaries and job security, for example—sometimes involving prestige and preference. In our society we generally feel that institutions that nurture "conflict of interest" frequently make bad policy—policy that supports the welfare of those with the conflict of interest not the welfare of the entire institution.

We have discovered that although many principled people are able to make selfless decisions, it is wiser to ask a legislator not to vote on a bill in which he or she has a substantial financial interest. We ask judges to excuse themselves from making decisions on cases in which they or their families are directly involved. We urge doctors not to practice medicine on themselves or their close kin. Aspirin, yes; surgery, no. In our country we long ago made the decision that basic policy decisions about war and peace should be made by civilians not generals.

The Anticlerical Option

In the churches we have built a system of ownership and decision making that institutionalizes conflict of interest. At various times Christians have tried to get around this problem in the church by eliminating clergy. The answer, these people say, is anticlericalism. Some denominations have attempted to install this answer. Most attempts to redefine or eliminate the clergy role have not been successful; time and again the role of the clergyperson has reemerged functionally, perhaps in a new form. Even John Milton, after a generation of experience with a newly defined "presbyter," was forced to admit that "new presbyter is but old priest writ large." Since World War II many denominations (United Methodist, Baptist, Brethren, Mennonite) that traditionally encouraged laity to carry leadership of congregations have systematically replaced them with professionally trained clergy. Even most Quakers now have chosen to have ordained clergy leadership.[7]

Religious Authority and the Clergy Role: Constructive and Demonic

As I have worked with many congregations of many denominations, I have found those trained and ordained into clergy roles generally to have had enormous ability to facilitate religious growth. (I must admit some bias—perhaps conflict of interest—because I have been an ordained clergyman for forty years.) Not all of those ordained are wise, not all use power well, not all are open to change or even to criticism, but for each I characterize negatively, I know dozens if not scores who simply and directly work to lead people to God, stand beside those in pain and suffering, encourage men and women to their best, lift them up when they are broken and lost, walk with them in the valley shadow; they raise questions about life-denying public or private actions, and in their own lives witness to the following of a higher calling. Most clergy I know understand and accept sacrificial living as their personal vocation. I am genuinely proud to be numbered with them.

I have noted in the dialogue between clergy and laity something far beyond rationality and pure expedience. The relationship has deep psychological and religious dimensions and powerful emotions dwell there. Over many generations this dialogue has had enormous capacity to foster growth and spiritual development.

Twenty years ago when I met Bruce Reed of the Grubb Institute of London, I first found some of this mystery and wonderful depth explained in a way that made sense.[8] Drawing insights from anthropology (especially Victor Turner), psychology (W. R. Bion and John Bowlby), and developmental theory (D.W. Winnicott), Reed analyzed the role of clergy in relationship to the spiritual life of the individual Christian and the life of the institution. In short, the "religious person" carried great emotional authority. The role of the person or place habitually associated with the presence of the holy had a critical part in how a believer appropriated the benefits of any renewed sense of identity and purpose.

In more recent years the issue of the authority of the clergy role has become more familiar to us for the worst of reasons; we have discovered in very public ways that many clergy have misused that role, abusing those around them in many ways, often, tragically, for sexual exploitation. The authority of the role is so great that it can be used manipulatively for selfish purposes, victimizing others. The authority of the role can turn the dialogue between clergy and lay into demonic and destructive patterns.

The demonic use of the role of the clergy demonstrates the *potential* for positive growth. In healthy dialogue between clergy and the laity, the authority inherent in the clergy role has the potential for healing, for nurture, for challenge, and for self-discovery. The novels of Graham Greene go further, suggesting that the power for good in the role of the clergyperson is present even in the most undeserving carriers, echoing a traditional belief of the church that the power is not limited by the virtue (or lack of it) of the person bearing it.

It is not unlike the power inherent in the role of a father or mother—which has the potential for permanently infantilizing the child or conversely calling the child to maturity. One does not argue to abolish parents because some parents use the role poorly. People I know see the creative potential in parental roles and seek to grow better parents. So it is—or should be—with clergy.

Creative dialogue between clergy and laypeople has enormous potential for being the locus for pastoral care and development. It can be an important tool in the equipping of the saints for their ministries.

Another View: Clergy as Overfunctioners

Edwin A. Friedman[9] and his colleagues[10] in the field of family process have given us language and a framework by which we can visualize another danger to the potentially creative dialogue between clergy and the laity. Family process describes how those in helping relationships are tempted to assume responsibility for others' lives. In attempting to help someone out of a bad patch of one kind or another, the helper makes decisions or directs behavior that should be made and directed by the person in trouble. By rationalizing his or her actions as "help" for one who is "helpless," the helper only serves to create dependency and provide the person in trouble with an excuse to abdicate personal authority. Friedman defines "overfunctioning" as taking over from the person in trouble; "underfunctioning" is the dependent behavior of that same person. Continued over time,, these patterns of behavior create a class of overfunctioners and an underclass of underfunctioners, and the conditions themselves become chronic and self-replicating.

The relationship between clergy and the laity over the years has built chronic overfunctioning into the role of the clergy and underfunctioning into the role of the laity. The clergy has come to expect the laity to underfunction, and the prophecy is self-fulfilling. The laity has come to expect the clergy to overfunction, and this, too, is self-fulfilling. Neither finds it easy to challenge the depressingly self-replicating pattern of dependence.

A Prophetic Role: The Interim Pastor—Powerless but Having Authority

More than two decades ago colleagues and I began exploring an alternative without at first realizing what we were dealing with. Our driving purpose at the time was to discover how to make a creative change when one pastor left a congregation and another was installed. We knew that some such changes were unusually traumatic for everyone involved. When there had been a particularly bad fight, perhaps with a long history of contentious relations between clergy and laity in a congregation, we discovered that the congregation's next pastorate was often short and miserable, even disastrous, replicating all the negatives of the previous experience. Similarly we found that a particularly long pastorate—fifteen years or more—was often fairly creative, but that the church's subsequent pastorate was marked by an unusually large number of unsatisfying experiences. As we identified these special cases where problems seemed to arise when one pastor was quickly replaced with another, we saw a need for a time of healing or pausing. We also discovered that the churches were raising up a few pastors whose instincts made them a natural to go into such situations for the "in-between time."

From this special cadre of pastors we identified needed skills and learned how to train what we started calling the interim pastor. This is a title and a role now widely established and used in many denominations. We have trained talented people specifically for short-term pastoral leadership roles. These pastors have become specialists in clearing out the underbrush left over from former experiences, helping congregations get ready for another long-term pastoral relationship. Our research showed that when the interim role was done well, the next installed pastor seemed to have a higher chance of success.[11]

In identifying this new role of interim pastor, we had stumbled onto a kind of religious leadership and pastoral authority that circumvented the "ownership" issue. By being intentionally a short-term actor in the congregation's life, the interim pastor was freed of the long-range responsibility for the future of the congregation—a responsibility generally felt deeply by pastors installed permanently. Ownership was not an issue to or with the interim pastor.

The interim pastor understood that he or she was to provide limited, temporary help in a congregation by entering a system in which ministry

with integrity was already "happening," in which there was a long history of ministry. The assumption and the contract of the interim pastor
called for the position to be temporary.

Within the interim period the psychological contract of both pastor
and congregation changed. The interim pastor was understood to be the
religious leader, encouraging and strengthening local leadership. The
responsibility for the life of ministry in that place did not belong to the
interim pastor but to the laity.

I must admit, however, that the old model of pastorate is so deeply
ingrained in the laity and the clergy that most "permanent" pastors, when
installed, resurrect the old patterns of overfunctioning clergy and underfunctioning laity.

Without fully understanding what we were doing, my colleagues and
I had developed a model of ministry that was not locked into the "overfunctioning" standard model. Simply by acknowledging the temporary
nature of the role, we placed the pastor and congregation in different
roles of ownership, different relationships of authority, and opened the
doors to fully functioning roles of laity in ministry and of clergy in
ministry.

Since I have understood the dynamics of what we did, I have been
trying to teach all pastors that they are interim pastors, even if they stay
in place for thirty years. On this point I have won a few battles—and lost
many more. The old pattern will not change easily. The standards set and
the instincts trained in the clericalist model are resistant to change.   ·

This "interim mentality" is the most direct clue I have had as to how
we can change the ownership issue. Where it has worked, the clergy have
found new freedom and authority to be the religious leaders they want to
be and the laity have discovered new ways in which their ministry is
fully owned by themselves, not continually dependent upon the clergy.

Conclusion

I began this chapter calling for a change of ownership in the church.
Such a call is not a function of anticlericalism; it is simply a statement
that the churches cannot be fully and effectively in ministry in the twenty-
first century by continuing patterns inherited from the twentieth.

I believe there must be a new dialogue between clergy and laity, a dialogue in which neither seeks to lord it over the other, neither defers to the other, but both give their best to the relationship. It will be a relationship in which the historic power of the role of religious authority is claimed and taken on without apology by those we probably will continue to call clergy. It will also be a relationship in which those we now call laity will see themselves as fully functioning colleagues, standing on their own feet and assured of the authenticity of their witness and work.

In the process of building religious institutions, we have created a power and ownership structure in which the clergy wields most of the power. They are now trapped in that role by history and by the arrangements locked in place by customs and laws intended to preserve the institution. In fact, the "arrangements" keep the clergy in institutional power but make it increasingly impossible for individual clergy to carry out their mandate to be bearers of the religious mystery, to have religious rather than institutional authority.

The task of the next generations will be to shift the power and ownership structures of the churches to allow laypeople to fulfill their apostolic ministries and, in so doing, free the clergy to be the catalysts of religious authority.

CHAPTER 2

CHALLENGE 2:
To Find New Structures
to Carry Our Faith

The institutional framework of our churches is no longer working. So far, we have not been able to build a framework that is adequate for the years ahead.

The second challenge in building churches for the future is to construct new institutional structures that can carry the faith to generations yet to be born.

In my first book about the future of the church, I described many places in which our institutions do not work, and I described some of the historical reasons for the breakdown.[1]   In my second book on the subject, I said little about structures.[2] There I focused on the functions the church of the future needs to embody, not the form of the embodiment. Now I want to return to structural issues, believing them to be one of our critical challenges.

Note that I make a big assumption here: I believe that structures are necessary to carry truth from one generation to another. I am aware of some "movements" (such as Alcoholics Anonymous) that perpetuate themselves with seemingly little or no structural form. And I am familiar with the argument that faith is more a movement than an institution. But as I review the history of the church, I see that most new insights that have survived to a second or third generation have found enough *structure* to outlive the one who generated the insight. And I note that my own generation received the faith through structures that, though flawed, had the ability to pass on truth from former generations.

It is also true that every generation is tempted to preserve the structures rather than the insights of the previous generation. When that temptation wins out, the critical task is to break through the structures and help the insights—if they are still viable—find structures more adequate for a new time.

That is the task we now face. The forms and structures of our churches have served well to bring the truths of the faith to this generation, but they have also become so calcified and rigid that they block communication of the insights of faith.

Many kinds of structures are needed to carry any movement from one generation to the next, and the church is no exception to this. The church must find organizational structures and structures of community that can enhance communication with the new generation—any new generation.

Our effort to meet this challenge of new structures is made more difficult by the fact that we are used to changing our structures very slowly, if not almost imperceptibly. We have grown accustomed to a pace that allows a decade or two—or even three, if necessary—to change a hymnal or book of worship. We have never before lived in a rapidly changing world where societal changes demand a quick response. We have never dealt with the need for rapid structural change, so we do not have very good adaptive mechanisms. We are in new territory.

Underlying Problems with our Denominational Structures

Today we are experiencing obvious pain in the organizational structures that make up our denominations: relationships among congregations, between congregations and their regional bodies (judicatories), between congregations and national bodies, and between regional and national bodies.

Issues of Trust

Many of us who are older remember when our denominational structures represented trusted, effective ways for different groups and interests within the denomination to work together for the mission goals we shared. Those denominational structures, led by bishops or executives, made it possible for the concerns or needs of one part of the denomination to be connected to concerns and needs in other regions. The structures made up a skill and resource delivery system that brought the whole life of the denomination to bear at the point of missional need. So trusted were those networks that people gave sacrificially to keep them operating, even when those networks were never able to do all the churches wanted to do. Most of us felt considerable loyalty to those relationships, and we were proud to be part of it all.

That sense of trust in the structures evaporated a long time ago. To be truthful, it evaporated in many other segments of our society—medicine, law, higher education, government, business—at about the same time. (What we are talking about is not just a phenomenon of the churches; we are experiencing a paradigm shift that touches every corner of our society in terms of an erosion in the authority of social structures or a loss of loyalty.)

Today's bishop or presbytery executive, district superintendent, or area minister often has to pacify a rebellious or angry constituency before beginning to work with them. An assumption of suspicion has replaced the assumption of trust. Congregations are now predisposed to resist whatever initiatives those in the "upper" structures propose, even when the proposals are first rate. This climate of distrust and suspicion severely handicaps communication and effective collaboration from the top down or from the bottom up.

No matter how hard the "upper" levels try to listen to the "grassroots," they are not perceived as being very attentive. The assumption of distrust makes neither party willing to allow the other to change behavior. Organizational paralysis can be the result.

I see the church already experimenting with new structural relationships. In many places individual congregations are taking on functions judicatories used to perform, such as program development and training. In some cases this is done almost in an adversarial stance to the judicatory. ("Anything you can do, I can do better," as Annie Oakley put it.) But I also see congregations collaborating with their judicatories, taking initiative and providing resources the judicatory does not provide. Networks of "training congregations" are emerging, providing a variety of educational programming and innovative liturgical and musical resources, much of it first class. Training initiated by these congregations usually reaches across several denominations. Such efforts to find new structures link our concerns to one another and allow us to help others and be helped by them.

Loss of Interdependence

Different levels within the same denomination do not work together as easily as they once did. The middle judicatory—diocese or conference or presbytery—stands awkwardly in-between the local congregation and the national structures. Lines of power and finance get tangled up. Congregations, heavily pressured by their own finances, try to respond to the judicatory's needs while the judicatory is "squeezed" by responsibility for national needs. From time to time totally new agencies or groups, some of them regional or ecumenical, enter the competition seeking support and participation. The congregations' cries for financial relief or program assistance grow louder, yet the national structures are importunate in demanding resources and money to meet emerging new mission issues. In fact, the needs at each level have great legitimacy, but often far outstrip the resources available. Unhealthy competition and feelings of betrayal and abandonment are more frequent than one would wish. There is little sense of interdependence upon one another.

Denominations do not work easily with other denominations at any level. The happiest relationships are probably local, where numbers of congregations seem able to get together to take on local initiatives without worrying about all the denominational furniture. Food banks, homeless shelters, Meals-on-Wheels, retirement home ministries—all are ways in which congregations of different denominations collaborate regularly. Regionally, judicatories of various denominations seem intent on running duplicative efforts that frequently seem worse than useless.[3]

Because of budget constraints and staff cutbacks in most so-called mainline denominations, program production and resourcing from the national offices have become almost nonexistent.

Regional and national judicatories have major changes to make if they are to be part of the picture of the church in the middle of the twenty-first century. Elsewhere I have argued for the critical importance of the middle judicatory,[4] but the case for the true and necessary functions of the national structures is yet to be made. Clearly such a case must be made before we can determine how much or what is needed in national organizational structures. It is unfortunate that the shortage of money adds to the pressure on these levels. The need to redesign and cut back at the same time has pushed for short-term adjustments and the defending of turf. Little time has been available for the basic structural redesign that is needed.

Perhaps the most difficult task of all will be to build trust among the elements of the structures we develop. This will take time, but it will not begin until the "higher" levels learn to listen to the "lower" levels or until each level quits making the others the perennial scapegoats.

Financial Issues

One other element of our problem of organizational structure needs to be noted, and I suspect that this element is behind most of the trouble. The financial system undergirding our denominations is in catastrophic trouble. If the church is to be a church in the future, it will need to build a new financial model. Let me name two specific financial issues that we must work through.

1. Our method of funding regional, national, and other structures depends upon gathering resources in the local congregation, then freely giving them to the various offices in loyalty and in support of the wider mission of the church. Thus from the flow of resources toward mission, each level of the church received enough funding to cover its essential costs. But as funds get tight, that flow is impeded, slowed, and in some cases stopped. In a new paradigm of mission in which the local mission is expanding in importance, there is no longer the compellingly obvious need to send funds "up the ladder." More funds are being kept locally, while everything outside the congregation loses income. Funds held locally are not all held for local mission; costs of local congregations have been rising much more rapidly than other church costs. If that weren't enough, all the agencies that used to be strongly supported by regional or national funds—seminaries, mission agencies, even church program units—now go directly to congregations to make a pitch for support. The result is "designated giving," often another name for cutting the contribution to the regional and national budgets. Here is the structural challenge: How do we determine the *essential* functions of regional and national judicatories, and how do we pay for them if that "bottom-up" financial system no longer works? Should those services be provided only when and where they are paid for by the user? What about congregations that cannot pay? How much of the regional and national structure do we need, and for what? Is this a new reason to develop regional and national endowments? How do we determine what is essential regionally and nationally, and how do we pay for it?

2. The economic model of the local congregation is already out of reach for half the congregations in our country; the cost of upkeep for a "standard-model" congregation far exceeds the means of half our congregations. In spite of this, many judicatories have plans afoot to open new congregations as rapidly as possible on this "standard" model. I am reminded of the story of the man who found it cost fifty cents to make a widget that he could not sell for more than forty cents. His solution to the problem was to increase the output of widgets so as to increase sales. Yes, he went bankrupt faster than he otherwise would have. But he had great sales for a while. Let me show you how this model works in real life by caricaturing what we do. You might call this sketch "How the Church 'Really Works.'" Please remember that this is a caricature; it exaggerates reality far beyond what any of us have experienced so that we can recognize what we often do not want to see.

I will describe a mythical judicatory. (If you are Episcopal or Catholic, call this a diocese; if Presbyterian, a presbytery; if United Methodist or United Church of Christ, a conference; if Lutheran, a synod—you get the idea!)

The Diocese of Midlandia (as I'm an Episcopalian, we'll use my language) is like lots of other judicatories. It covers a geographic region that includes several cities and towns and the suburban-exurban areas like those that are in your own judicatory. As a religious structure, here's how it works. There are half a dozen really big churches. Everybody knows them. They are the "plums" that most of the clergy are dying to get called to. They have big budgets and fine buildings. They have excellent music, imaginative worship, and their educational programming is first rate. Each has a strong staff. Some of them, over the years, have been on the conservative side of a lot of issues; others much less so. These are the congregations you can count on. Strong, vibrant. (I don't want to be romantic about it; one or two of them may, from time to time, treat their clergy or their bishop just awfully, and they can be stubborn and mean-spirited, too, but on the whole they are fine places.)

But Midlandia has a lot of fine smaller congregations, too. They are the "ordinary" variety: one pastor on the staff, sometimes a full- or part-time secretary. Many of them are marvelous places for worship and education, places where the members have a great sense of community with one another. Like the "plums," some of these have problems from time to time; indeed, several years of conflict may almost break their backs. But week by week, good stuff happens—people are nurtured and go about trying to make a difference in their community. Some of these congregations struggle every year to come up with the resources for the annual budget, but usually they make it.

Midlandia also has a flock of quite small congregations that never quite seem to "make it." Although they have marvelous members, as a group they are always feeling a bit put-down because they have to ask for grants from the diocese and sometimes they aren't able to meet their obligations. Most of them have to share a pastor with another place, or, what may be more common, they have to make sure their pastor does not stay too long. If a pastor stays more than two or three years, they run out of funds to pay the salary. During the gaps between pastors, they put money in the bank to help pay future bills. Most of these congregations are used to hand-to-mouth existence. Although they are aware of the way the rest of the diocese tends to look down on them, some of them take pride in being "different." I remember going to the anniversary of one of these congregations, celebrating two and a half centuries of being a subsidized congregation.

As I draw this caricature of Midlandia, you may want to give names to the congregations of your judicatory who fit the categories:

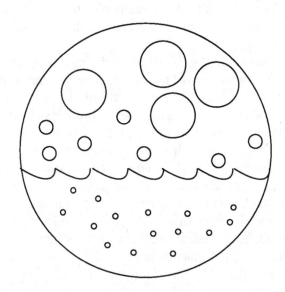

Note the wavy line I drew across the picture. It represents financial solvency.

Above that line, congregations "make it." Below it, some form of subsidy is needed to keep the congregations going. It is almost as if that wavy line is a "water line." Above it, the congregations are in the fresh air. Below it, the congregations are "under water."

How do we tend to manage this problem? We have discovered that the plums and the midsized congregations have some "extra" resources. If we use the air analogy, they have a bit more—some of them have lots more—than they need to sustain their own existence. That's where regional judicatories come in. We have come to see judicatory offices as places to which we can send the excess air from the stronger congregations, a kind of pumping station. We set up a "hose" from the judicatory office down to the tiny subsidized congregations, and we pump just enough air down to keep them alive.

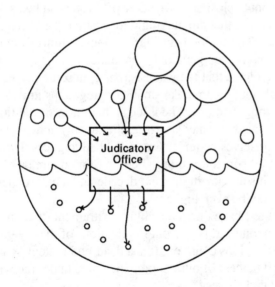

Of course this is absurd, but bear with me. And to tell the truth, doesn't it point to some of the ways we behave?

This caricature is kept alive by two fictions.

The first is our official party line: We say that all the tiny congregations really can grow up to be like the plums. But we know in our heart

of hearts that this is not true. We have rarely seen this happen to dependent congregations. Occasionally one may explode, perhaps when the
suburbs of the nearby city stretch in, or when a major corporation sets up
a new plant in the community. But we know it is very rare for this to
happen. In fact, only one person doesn't know this whole thing is a fiction: the young seminary student sent out there, encouraged to believe
that by her or his efforts this little village mission can become a cathe-
dral. Too many young pastors' hearts and spirits have
been broken by trying to do that.

The other fiction is destructive on a larger scale. It says that the congregations above the water level are not affected by the water; that the
water inevitably will dry up and the small and large congregations will
flourish together. Operating under this fiction, the large and middle-sized
congregations often feel very philanthropic and religious, "helping" all
those "poor congregations." That is, they feel that way until they have a
few tight budget years and begin murmuring about all those "subsidies"
and muttering about "closing down some of those dead beats." The fiction encourages those that are making it to separate themselves from
those that are not. The fiction keeps large congregations from understanding that they, too, are genuinely threatened.

You see, the fact is that the water is rising. In some places it is rising
fast. The issue is not how to make small congregations grow into large,
self-sustaining congregations. The issue is that many of the fine middle-
sized congregations that today are struggling to stay above water by tomorrow will themselves be under water. If I had to guess, I would pre-
dict that at least 20 percent of those single-pastor congregations will be
threatened with insolvency in the next decade and a half. Others tell me
the proportion may be even higher.

The caricature I have drawn is a blunt instrument. It is not very
subtle. By exaggeration it points out implications of the organizational
structures congregations count on. It is a dead-end system. Right now
perhaps 40 to 50 percent of our congregations are under the water line.
More are going under every year.

I trust this caricature helps readers recognize the organizational dead
end we face. You see, there is no way out of what I have described. To
survive in the next century, most congregations will have to learn to
breathe water. Continuing to spend energy learning better air-breathing
methods, continuing to start new congregations on the old economic
model—both of these are dead ends.

Breathe water? Impossible? Of course it is. I mean there is no way that creatures such as we can learn in our lifetimes to grow gills and webbed hands and feet and learn to live underwater. There is no way we can make it by learning to hold our noses and take deeper breaths when we get to the surface.

A whole new kind of existence is called for if we physically were to learn to breathe water. That's precisely what this caricature calls for in terms of our basic church structure. I am not talking about our learning how to tinker with our congregational system, to find out how to make it work a bit better. The organizational structures we now have are broken irreparably, and things of a totally new order need to be developed. New church planting, so long as we are planting the same kind of thing that's failing now in more than half the cases, is not enough, and it may be wrong.

One thing I like about the caricature is what it can do to our perception of the small, dependent congregation. As things are now, of course, they are the drag on the system. The failures. The ones that can't quite make it.

But if we are serious about learning how to breathe water, look at what some of those congregations have been doing! Most have been experimenting with water breathing for years. Many have learned to maintain fine congregational life and life-affirming ministry without full-time staff. They have learned to generate financial resources out of nothing. They know how to get blood out of turnips, or at least how to get enough turnips to trade in on a blood transfusion.

No thanks, however, to the rest of the churches! The system we have is not helping these congregations. Rather, it is training them in dependence. Many are being damaged by the efforts of the rest of the church to "help" them, which amounts to leaching all of their imagination out of them. The longer we continue the dependency system I have caricatured above, the more damage we will do them and the less they will have to offer as pioneers in breathing water.

I do not want to be romantic about these congregations. With their tenacity, they have the potential to be pioneers for us—if we have not damaged them too badly. Those congregations in the midsized range that will slide below the water line in the next decade are going to need a lot of help. So far, I see no initiatives that have wholehearted denominational backing by the denominations to help with that problem. Some individual regional judicatories are experimenting, but they are swimming against the current.[5]

We desperately need pioneers to search out new economic models for the work of the church. We need local congregations operating with less than full-time staff and congregations that see that as the best way to do mission and ministry. We need congregations with the courage to merge their operations with others, not necessarily of the same denomination or even faith group. We need more pioneers who will help congregations learn to use and provide services on an entrepreneurial basis and teach us how to get help to those who cannot afford it. We need to learn how to help a self-sustaining congregation adjust to a lesser role without losing its sense of integrity and mission.

The Ecumenical Part of Our Structural Challenge

Researchers are telling us that fewer and fewer members of our denominations are content to be dyed-in-the-wool members of their own denomination, come what may. There is a fairly constant flow of ordinary members from one denomination to another. Younger Americans seem to have more ecclesiastical wanderlust than their elders. (Clergy remain pretty consistently denominational, perhaps influenced by the difficulty of switching credentials and pensions from one denomination to another.)

Let's be honest. Most of our denominational differences represent territorial and theological feuds now three or four hundred years old. Relics of those feuds have been preserved in our organizational structures the way an insect may be preserved in a bead of amber. The reasons for the feud were very real, and the arguments we use today to defend our positions are genuine, but in most cases the arguments have to do with what happened a long time ago. In the life of the Catholic Church of his time, Martin Luther saw some practices and beliefs that caused him to start a revolution that resulted in the formation of the Lutheran churches. But to tell the truth, one would be hard put to find a region of the Catholic Church today (certainly not in the United States) where Catholic practice and belief is what it was when Luther took offense. I have not heard of the sale of a single indulgence in the past decade! Nearly every Catholic service I attend uses the hymn "A Mighty Fortress Is Our God." I hear it more there than I do in Lutheran churches. Indeed it would be hard to find a nickel's worth of difference between most of the denominations in basic theological principles today. Practices? Oh, yes. Catholics play bingo and Anglicans have bazaars. And customs? Yes, again. Assemblies of God put a high stake on tithing and Presbyterians "pledge."

I do not mean to trivialize the genuine differences that remain (the issue of the ordination of women truly is a significant difference), but the ordinary church member finds the rationale for those differences increasingly trivial. The differences are much less central to the faith community than they were in the past. Our institutional structures formed around an "allergic reaction." We seem to have lived long enough to have become desensitized to what caused the original reaction. Meanwhile we have not and do not change our behavior.

What is true of the Lutherans and Catholics is true of most of the other denominational groupings. You sometimes find a Presbyterian who still goes apoplectic at the word *bishop,* and you will find Episcopalians who still mutter about "the enormities of the bishop of Rome," but you will not get a war going. And remember—most of the differences that started our denominations started physical combat in their time.

Look at the more important goals of the denominations today—their mission agenda. Each is struggling to rethink international mission agenda in light of a changed international scene and shortages of funding. Each is concerned for caring for the homeless and hungry in our society. Each worries about those who are excluded from society. Each is working on what "ministry of the laity" means and what that has to do with the role of the clergy. Each is trying to find out how better to educate its clergy.

Each is trying to learn how better to deal with ethnic diversity. Each is struggling to come to terms with major changes in human behavior—particularly sexual. Each is trying to overcome the built-in racism in its community. Each is struggling to find how to distribute power more justly and to recognize those who have been disenfranchised in the past. Each is trying to learn how to balance modernist and traditional theological articulations. Each is living with an internal civil war between "liberals" and "conservatives" with the terms defined in terms of the American political agenda more than theological positions.[6]

In terms of basic belief and practice, the differences among the denominations are more and more negligible. In terms of what the denominations are trying to do, the differences are even more negligible.[7]

What's left to be different about, except aesthetics and memory? Canadian, Reginald Bibby suggests that our denominations may become more like families or clans, places where we can celebrate common history and tradition, communities in which we can express our special kinship with one another and even do those things we have done peculiarly over the generations, such as Anglican chant and Presbyterian psalmody, Baptist gospel songs and Methodist "fellowships." We may come less and less to need our denominations as bastions from which we defend ultimate principles from the satanic forces of the "others."

Compared to where denominational differences were just a half century ago, we already are "like family." Protestant pastors in training read Catholic theologians, and Catholics return the compliment. None of that would have occurred fifty years ago.

The structures that separate us denominationally do not yet reflect the lowering of boundaries that has already happened. In the next generation we need to find ways to increase our communication across those boundaries. This is one area in which deregulation is long overdue. It might have happened already if those with the greatest stake in the status quo—the clergy—were not the primary speakers in the ecumenical dialogues between denominations.

Interfaith Structures?

The boundaries between denominations are nothing compared to the boundaries between Christian churches and other faith groups. I believe those interfaith boundaries also need to be redrawn in the next generation.

Relationships between Christian churches and other faiths were set in stone in a period I have called the Age of Christendom.[8] That age assumed that history was moving toward a consummation in which all humanity would be united in the church; all the other faiths would wither away. Even in the earliest times, Paul struggled with this assumption when others asked him "What of the Jews who have not accepted Christ?" Paul's stumbling answer indicated his quandary. He did believe that all were called to become part of the church, but he also recognized the empirical fact that many Jews chose to continue a faith-life within their own tradition. Paul never solved the issue, nor did successive generations of Christians. At the time of the Enlightenment, the Christendom assumption that all would eventually come into the church came to be linked with Western European political and economic power. The result was the integration of cultural, political, and religious triumphalism into what we called imperialism. The militaristic hymns of the late nineteenth century cast interfaith relations as warfare, with the power of God leading the church's armies against the heathen.

We are heirs to an understanding of the church that is filled with all kinds of cultural imperialism. Even though the world view of Christendom no longer holds sway, its relics remain in our thinking. Emotionally we believe in and sing about a triumph of the church over all the "lesser" faiths. Many of us do not want those militaristic hymns removed from our hymnbooks—because they are familiar, because they were taught to us when we were young. But we also sing them because they reflect the only relationship between Christianity and other faiths that our parents knew. It represented an honored—if flawed—world view. Those hymns expressed a fairly universal consensus of the churches that all other faiths were in retreat before the conquering hosts of the church, and that we would see the end of those faiths, probably in the "Christian century."

Many of us brought up on the militant hymns and a nineteenth-century model of mission simply compartmentalized our brains. With one part of our consciousness we hold on to the mission schema we learned years ago; with another part we register the fact that reality certainly has changed! Americans do not see the Moslem world fading away in the face of a triumphant church; they see a vigorous, diverse community of Moslem faith expanding in Africa and Asia and claiming more adherents in the United States than Presbyterians or Episcopalians! We see strong movements within other world religions that do not wither away as we, in our pride, might have thought they would. Americans are getting accustomed to seeing new religious buildings, e.g., mosques and Hindu temples, as they travel around their country.

In "Christendom" the relationship of Christians to those of other faiths was clear. "Convert them or kill them." Not many people I know today are content with that model. It may be analogous to how sixteenth-century Lutherans felt about Catholics or seventeenth-century Presbyterians felt about Anglicans. In the denominations we no longer act on or even believe the hostility we once felt. Is it possible for Christians to move beyond nineteenth-century models of relationship to other faiths?

How can we discover a new way that affirms living alongside people of other faiths?

I believe there is room for hope in the way Christians and Jews have made the first, fateful steps toward mutual engagement. Perhaps triggered by the trauma of the Holocaust, Christians—not all of them, to be sure—have begun to reach toward a new and creative relationship with our Jewish cousins in faith. Christians have come to recognize how they have contributed to anti-Semitic thinking and actions. They have discovered deeply hurtful elements in their thinking and scriptures that have to be identified and confessed before new relationships can be built. But pioneers have been working on this boundary for several decades now. Today you can find rabbis and pastors meeting weekly to study the scriptures for mutual enlightenment.9 Laity of the two faiths are beginning to gather together for Bible study.

Participants in the interfaith conversations, the study groups, and the formal conferences affirm new learnings and new depths of understanding of their own faith family. The conversations that seemed risky by an old understanding of our mission have proven to be spiritually enriching to both families of faith.

The challenge of finding new structures for the future includes finding structures that build new nonimperialistic relationships with the resurgent world religions. As churches we must put behind us a model of mission that has strong emotional ties to our past—a model of mission built in and nurtured by the Age of Christendom, which is no more. The church of the future is called to stand beside and with other world faiths, not over them. That will not come easy for us because we have identified so much of who and what we are with a triumphal stance in society, a stance that could be understood in the terms of the Age of Christendom, but which makes no sense in the age that is emerging.

In the past we understood our role in the world to be "ruler." Can we embrace a role in which we stand in solidarity with those of other faiths? Can we understand our own faith to be large enough and secure enough not to have to lord it over others?

Conclusion

Building new structures is the second challenge to the future.

The challenge for new structures touches the commonplace: how we put our organizations together in new ways, how we find ways to finance those structures. Our challenge is to rethink how we engage one another within the denominational structures we have now and how we adapt those structures.

At a deeper level, as we consider our life with those of other faiths, we realize that we are being called not just to tinker with structures, but to dig into the heart of what we have called "mission" and to find new reality for that old word, perhaps letting go of some of our favorite things.

Our ability to open ourselves to this conversation with God and to trust God's leading will be a measure of our willingness to take on the role of pioneer for the church of the future. Please remember. Many pioneers get lost. But if they do not go out in front and blaze trails, other people will not find their way.

This is the second challenge I am laying before us: finding new structures to carry our faith.

CHAPTER 3

CHALLENGE 3:
To Discover a Passionate Spirituality

I expect that most readers of this book will find the title of this chapter startling, if not offensive. There is a story behind it. I genuinely believe that the churches must discover a passionate, even charismatic, spirituality. Stay with me as I tell my story.

Connecting Knowledge of God with Experience of God

I grew up in a wonderful parish, although in later years I could recognize its faults. The congregation sustained me and many others. The life of the place taught many of its worshippers truths beyond what was actually said and done. That ability of a congregation to proclaim more than it consciously knows is a bedrock of my monomania for congregations.

In that parish I rarely came across the word or the idea of *spirituality*. It was assumed that any needed nourishment was provided in the ordered structures of the worship and preaching. On Christmas and Easter that ordinary, ordered worship "ascended" to a heightened intensity. I lived with a "cool" spirituality. It had a depth and power that helped people through enormous trials and carried them through long hard journeys that tested them in every way. It was a spirituality that held them together in the face of tragedy and went with them into the valley of the shadow. It was a real spirituality. A real sense of firsthand communion with God. But it was a spirituality that nobody much talked about. What I learned about this kind of growing into God was surrounded by "oughts": how one ought to pray; how one cleansed oneself for communion with God. The way to God was a long, difficult road that

I learned about. It was a road with many detours—on which I seemed to be most of the time. There was not a lot of joy associated with the walk.

My experience in theological seminary reinforced this view of spirituality. Knowing and being close to God was described and analyzed but rarely witnessed to or experienced. I got more detailed road maps and a clearer sense of the blocks we set up to spiritual growth. I learned several different approaches to spiritual growth—what steps to take and the characteristics of different ways. With all the description and analysis, however, I remember only one teacher who said to me—in a one-on-one conversation—"Let me tell you what I do." Even in seminary, spirituality—being connected with God—was similar to that which I had experienced in my parish. It was the "understood," the "assumed" piece that everyone knew to be at the heart of the religious enterprise but that nobody talked about directly, except in a lecture.

I think that would not have been enough for me without a parallel range of experiences that connected my head with my heart. I look back on a number of critical moments and turning points in my childhood and young adult years. They often occurred when least expected. Outwardly they were not very remarkable. I remember moments in the middle of the ordered Sunday worship of my parish when I was seized by something beyond myself. And other times when I was simply blown away with feelings I could not voice. I remember as a child discovering what absolution meant in the presence of a black Baptist woman who cleaned our house. I remember moments during evensong at church camp when the Voice I heard was not that of the campers and other counselors. I remember moments of quiet when I experienced "being-outside-myself" and in a greater Presence. I remember a time of great fear in which Someone gave me hopeful words from a psalm. I remember learning to pray as a young clergyman with two men who were each three times my age. (If my memory is selective, so be it—there were and are so many moments in which the Presence was present.)

Years later I found some colleagues who shared a fascination with the spiritual dimension of life. Three of them were intrigued by a research concept I floated by them in 1972—that we try to discover, on an empirical basis, what "spiritual growth" looked like.[1] Unbeknownst to us, Jean Haldane was pursuing a similar research project within a single parish. Our complementary projects involved one-on-one interviews, asking people to tell the story of their religious life. Both reports were published, with the Haldane document remaining in print for more than a decade.[2] What did we learn? First, that everyone we talked to could describe powerful, personal experiences with God. The experiences were unique to the individual but all very real. Some of them had occurred in a "religious" setting, but most had not. Many had been life-changing events. Second, we learned that none of the people who told us of these experiences had ever been asked to tell his or her story to his or her congregation or pastor, and none had ever thought of bringing it up. It was as if the churches and parishioners had an implicit understanding that experiences did not matter in the church or to the church. It felt to us like a collusion of silence.

We researchers found it strange to discover such a gulf between people's experience of God and the congregational structures—even though the congregations had given the people words to explain those experiences, the images with which to recognize whom they had met, and even opened them to receive the experience. They used images they had learned in church to describe their experiences to us. Yet at the same time, knowledge of God and experience with God had somehow become completely different realities for these people. There seemed to be two worlds—the world in which one relates to God formally and another in which one is personally touched by the Spirit of God in the midst of ordinary life.

The Holy Spirit has always represented something unruly to the people of the church. People who love God and love the church are always discovering that the Holy Spirit paints outside the lines we draw to order our church life.

For two thousand years the church has staunchly organized and structured itself. It has engaged in complex theological struggles to clarify what it meant about God and who Jesus was and how he related to God. But the Holy Spirit remains the unacknowledged guest at the feast, at least partly because things get unpredictable when the Spirit is around.

What I have described—both my personal experience and what we saw as the experience of those who told us their stories—is related to the discomfort of structured religion around the unpredictable power of the Spirit who comes and goes without regard to our plans.

Historical Perspective

Throughout the history of the church the activity ascribed to the followers of the Spirit has caused contention and uncertainty. Writing of those who had the "gift of tongues," Paul gave such mixed signals that we suspect he would have been happier if he hadn't had to deal with them.[3] Paul clearly recognized the gift of tongues as a gift of the Spirit, and even though he claimed the gift himself, it seems he didn't particularly like it. He implied that almost anything else would have been better.

Rational plans and organizational structures always conflict with spontaneity. Where the Spirit comes and goes, spontaneity is to be expected. Organization wonks need to have things clear and orderly. Where the Spirit appears, the lines of demarcation get broken down; what is so carefully defined and structured seems to be a way for us to attempt to limit or control the urgent purposes of God.

Harvey Cox brings this age-old dilemma of the church into the twentieth century, describing the explosive impact of the contemporary charismatic movement across the globe.[4] He claims that Pentecostalism may be the one religious phenomenon that touches more Christians today than any other.

In the early years of this century a small church in Los Angeles became the location for the beginnings of what Pentecostals view as a new pouring out of the Spirit upon the world in our time.[5] This Azusa Street Revival quickly affected and challenged the ordered denominational systems of America and soon ignited a great global spiritual explosion.

At Azusa Street, and elsewhere as the movement spread to many parts of the country and overseas, men and women seemed able and willing to set aside conventional social barriers; black and white, male and female, young and old found common cause in the enthusiasm of their new-found exuberant faith—with the ancient practice of speaking in tongues as a common bonding experience. People danced and sang and praised God. The primary manifestations of the Spirit were explosive expressions of ecstasy, worship that did not fit the patterns of rational liturgies, healings, and singing and dancing—anything but the familiar, staid decorum most Christians knew to be the "correct ways" to address God.

This occurred at the very moment in history when Americans were moving toward more separations: Jim Crow laws were expanding; the distance between the sexes was widening. But in Los Angeles a whole new experience was born. As it spread across the country, it shattered the barriers polite society was trying to erect. No wonder it seemed revolutionary.

It was too much. The denominations and churches drew back from this vitality. Some who tried to bring the Azusa Street Revival into their denominations were not welcomed there. The Pentecostal denominations grew, sometimes splintering among themselves, finding it difficult to overcome society's divisiveness even among themselves. Mainliners scoffingly spoke of them as "holy rollers" and joked about their passionate expressions of faith.

Late in the sixties a new, somewhat sanitized version of charismatic renewal occurred within the mainline denominations. First reported in an Episcopal parish led by Dennis Bennett, this movement has spread into many of the denominations that rejected the Azusa Street experience. The second movement has been somewhat similar to the first, with considerable suspicion from "regular" churchgoers of these "far-out" people. The earlier denominational "blanket rejection" of the charismatic has not occurred, but I fear there lurks in both camps—charismatic and traditional—a hope that each could get rid of the other. Each seems to feel that the other is not only different, but wrong in some fundamental way.

I propose that the third challenge the churches must meet to build a church for the future is to find ways to bring this charismatic expression of spirituality into the heart of the Christian experience and bind it fully into the very structures and systems of the religious world of the churches. This will not be easy. Both "parties" seem to generate an allergic reaction in the other. Each acts as if the other is an essential threat.

Integrating the Gifts

Contrary to the behavior of the traditional mainliners and traditional charismatics, the challenge is not for one group to eliminate the other, but that the gifts of the ordered, structured approach to faith may be integrated into the vital, enthusiastic, Spirit-filled approach. The challenge is to move beyond the war between religious sensibilities and experiences to discover a new expression of faith that incorporates the gifts of both traditions.

Clearly there is tension between these forms of spirituality. Here I delineate their differences in list form, even though to do so oversimplifies reality and probably does injustice to both:

Traditional Spirituality	Charismatic Spirituality
Form is central	Experience is central
Structure is important. There are steps, procedures, practices to follow	Life is shaped by the free-flowing, free-moving Spirit; structures get in the way
Rational; subject to analytical thought	Emotional; analysis is irrelevant
Disciplined, ordered, patterned	Spontaneous, surprising
Measured, rhythmic (Mozart)	Profligate, multipatterned (jazz)
Self-effacing	Self-affirming
Can be diagrammed	Free-form, finger-painting
Unobtrusive	Overwhelming, obtrusive
Deep, often intense, quiet, private	Explosive, shattering, erupting, communal
Tenacious, steady	Unpredictable, mercurial
Frequently silent	Frequently loud, even raucous
Slowly and deeply burning (like long-lived underground fire in a volcano)	Explosive (like a pipe bomb)

These are more than lists of differences. Think of the people or groups you have known who express the best of each.

Followers of traditional spirituality have been people of great influence in my life. I think of people whose daily practice of disciplines of prayer sometimes seemed artificial to me but never to them. People who attended the mass daily before going to work. I find I am moved by essays and meditations that have grown out of weeks and months of thought and study, papers that witness to slow, steady growth in depth

and meaning. I am entranced by the careful, sometimes laborious statements of great theologians about the nature of God and humanity. I am
enlightened by the scrupulous work of anthropologists and scholars who
by painstaking analysis of bits and pieces of ancient cultures bring new
insight to my reading of the scriptures. I am moved often by the careful
liturgical planning and organization that lies behind a great occasion of
worship or celebration. Some are great moments of inspiration, built
upon long, sometimes dry periods of reflection and study. I am excited
by the language gift of those who can take an old truth and turn it inside
out—finding a new way to say it. I am grateful for the hands and knowledge of those who fix broken bones and cut out diseased tissue. I enjoy
the laborious work of the poet or hymnwriter whose art nourishes me in
reading and worship.

The best of the charismatic spirituality is equally life giving. There
is a "now-ness" to their perception of the presence of God that we traditionalists do not know well. I welcome the simple openness of the charismatic to what God is and can do. What a power of expectation is evident in hands uplifted in prayer and verbal affirmation in worship. I am
grateful for the wonderful charismatic woman who taught me from her
death-bed that one does not have to get well to be healed. I remember
moments that were great and dramatic because someone seized an opportunity no one else recognized, sensed the need of a situation, sensed
the call and power of God, and acted on faith, not on a predetermined
plan, not knowing for sure what the outcome would be.[6] As a "traditional" Anglican deeply imbued with the power of the Eucharist, I have
felt the new power released in the sacrament when the gift of tongues
was breathed over a large group as they sang after Communion. I have
seen lives transformed by God in places where I did not expect it to
happen. I have seen barriers broken down—separates brought together—
when it seemed impossible.

A church that does not find a way to include the liveliness of both
of these ways of spirituality is likely to miss something that God has in
store for us all. I venture further to say that neither side can be truly
healthy without the other in counterpoint. Each side deteriorates if left to
itself. The health of the one is dependent upon the health of the other. I
think that we see that as we look at what is happening in the churches
today.

When the traditional way of spirituality decays it becomes a stuffy, dry, lifeless formality. Many members of the traditional churches have lived in such a straitjacket of their tradition that they have never found the power available in that very tradition—consequently their lives quietly go rigid and dry. Outsiders looking to the church as a place to know God and be known by God see a spiritual desert, where people go through the motions of religion. Many members hold on and carry on, knowing they have had and hoping they may again have some of the experiences of grace that mark traditional spirituality at its best. And many others drift away, having given up hope. The younger generation, unwilling to pack its emotions in dry ice, simply opts for other venues in which to find vitality.

When charismatic spirituality decays, it goes in another direction. As in the case of traditional spirituality, it becomes a parody of its strengths. Charismatic spirituality at its worst degenerates into spiritual pride. It "puts down" any other experience of God as counterfeit. This characteristic of decayed charismatic spirituality often makes for severe conflict within congregations. This spirituality can also become uncritically supportive of any strong, assertive voice and can make peace with dictatorial leaders. It can deify the patterns of the past, both social and religious, forgetting the central promise that the Spirit will lead us into new truth. It sometimes moves beyond emotional vitality to an irrationality and a suspicion that are close to paranoia. The wholehearted dependence on God that characterizes the best of the charismatic life sometimes is unable to recognize gifts from God that do not fit what these believers expect God's gifts to be. They are not willing to admit that God paints outside the lines they recognize.

Two parallel lists, then, delineate two kinds of spirituality. Each can decay into something much less creative.

Our usual way of managing such differences is to see them as opposites and to treat them as a conflict of values or lifestyle, attempting to find out which is "better" and eliminating the other. We assume an either/or stance.

But both of these types of spirituality are essential to us. The machinery of the mainline denominations has been in the hands of the traditionalists for centuries with the result that the charismatic has been relegated to the fringe. To face the future, the church must find ways to bring the gifts of charismatic spirituality to the heart of the church life without denying the gifts and contributions of traditional spirituality. My hunch is that the presence of both, living in tension but not in opposition, will increase the vitality of both kinds of spirituality. Can we do that? Can we learn not only to tolerate each other (that's hard enough for many of us), but also to affirm and even sometimes love each other?

A colleague, Barry Johnson, has proposed a new way of looking at what we perceive to be opposites, a new way of bringing opposites into conversation with each other. In his challenging book *Polarity Management,* Johnson suggests that many differences are not true matters of conflict, where one must be eliminated for the other to survive.[7] He suggests a new "polarity" or "polar opposites," to describe a pair of differing realities that are both necessary. Like inhaling and exhaling, each is different from the other but both are essential to health.

I suggest that traditional and charismatic spirituality are polar opposites, and that the health of the body depends on our finding a creative way for them to coexist within the churches.

Johnson describes the way polar opposites need each other to maintain health. When traditional spirituality and charismatic spirituality are healthy and producing fruit in the lives of people, churches, and society, there is no problem. Neither will need to be negative about or defensive toward the other. Neither approach will be imperialistic, seeking to overthrow or undercut the integrity of the other.

The problem arises when either form of spirituality begins to decay. When the traditional decays into the dry, lifeless spiritual void, it grows more vulnerable and defensive; that's when it is most likely to fear or make enemies of those who approach spirituality in a different way. Similarly, when the charismatic approach decays into irrationality and sheer energy, it grows imperialistic, proud, and least able to live with anyone who has a different expression. Either spirituality under threat or sensing its own decay becomes defensive and least open to proponents of the other.

Johnson notes that as each pole degenerates into its lesser form, it grows more convinced that the only way "out" is to commit itself to its tradition and to try harder to make it work. The traditional form of spirituality, when it decays, assumes that the way to health is to reinforce traditional forms, patterns, and disciplines that once made sense and worked; when the formal structure stops providing sustenance, the best course is to try twice as much formal structure, spend more time in the forms that used to make sense. Johnson observes that it never works.

Such thinking drives the decayed truth deeper and deeper into decay and even into depression.

The same is true for the charismatic side of the polarity. The more it goes into decay, the more its worst characteristics come to the fore, and the more the unspoken command is given: Do it more; do it better. Again, it does not work. The decay goes on and "life" moves further and further away. The charismatic version of depression seems to be guilt.

Johnson's very helpful insight is that the way out of the decay of one polar reality is to be found only in the opposite pole. For example, as the traditional spirituality decays, it cannot be healed by working harder at the traditional way; it only digs itself deeper into its hole. Hope lies in seeking the positive gifts of charismatic spirituality, opening itself to experiencing the strengthening presence of the Spirit. Similarly, the decayed charismatic spirituality is not likely to find renewal simply in repeating the experiences that once gave life, but in seeking the gifts of the ordered, patterned, structured ways of spiritual development so familiar in the traditional forms.

Johnson's theory suggests a surprising prescription for someone for whom the traditional has become pedantic, dry, and routine: Seek out the totally different experience of charismatic spirituality. Immerse oneself there for a while and discover renewed vitality in the old forms. Similarly, for the charismatic beginning to feel guilty because that spirituality is not "working" very well: Take a silent retreat or meditate on the stations of the cross. In either case, the new experience can renew the vitality of one's spiritual path to God.

In Johnson's theories and research, I hear an affirmation of the debate in Paul about the nature of law and grace. Somehow the law holds us in bondage tighter and tighter, always making us think that the only way out is to try harder and harder to do what the law requires. The universal human experience is that this is a dead-end route. One either gives up in despair or cuts the law down to a manageable size. On their own, both forms of spirituality convince us that the only way is to go deeper in the way that has led us to despair.

Paul points to the fact that the answer is not to be found in the law, but in the reception of grace from outside. So those who have found life in either traditional or charismatic spirituality but have continued on to emptiness need to give up the hard-nosed attempt to overcome their emptiness by force of will. They need to allow another path to lead them back to health and wholeness.

Johnson describes a continuing oscillation between poles as the path of health. The Johnson theories give a framework for my proposal that the church is challenged to develop a larger spirituality than it has. As one whose home is in the traditional churches and forms of spirituality, I see an urgent need for those churches to open themselves to the charismatic dimension that they have kept at arms' length for two thousand years. For many in those families of churches, the aridity of the experience of religion is palpable. Those churches, while still mediating life to many in their pews, have generally ceased to be able to communicate to outsiders that they are repositories of living water.

It may be that the other need is as urgent: for those with the charismatic identity and experience to renew their connections to the traditional systems and structures of religious life. As one whose life has not been primarily in that community, I cannot judge its inner reality. But I see signs of what seem to an outsider to be a pride and narcissism that may represent a decay in portions of the charismatic community.

The long-term issue, regardless of who needs most at the moment, is whether or not we can build a sense of spiritual growth that embraces a wider spectrum of styles and methods, of experiences and structures. Because we cannot begin to imagine the challenges that will face those who will live in the twenty-first century, the spirituality we have—traditional or charismatic—will not suffice.[8] Perhaps those two great languages together can communicate living water in the deserts of the future.

CHAPTER 4

CHALLENGE 4:
To Feed the World's Need for Community

What and Where Is Community?

It was the summer of 1964. For ten months my family and I had been in England where I was an exchange pastor in a parish near London. We had enjoyed a warmth of hospitality that I have rarely experienced. I had attended family celebrations, and I had mourned with parishioners in their losses. When "our" president, John Kennedy, was assassinated, the entire village mourned with us, and many dropped by the house to bring flowers. We had worshipped together and, yes, we had pushed each other's understandings in many areas, not least of which was faith itself.

It had been a good year, but I was never able to let go of the sense of "home" I felt among the people of my family in South Carolina and my church family in North Carolina. High points of the year had been opening packages: My mother had air-mailed two pounds of grits to help us face the cold mornings of November. And my back-home choir had sent a tape of Christmas music that included a folk-song carol I particularly loved, "Jesus, Jesus, Rest Your Head," arranged by John Jacob Niles.

It was August. I was at a "pops" concert at Albert Hall in London, and I found myself sitting in that public place with tears streaming down my face. The music was a folk tune I knew from back home—the tune to the song "Going Home" (and the largo movement of Dvorak's "Fifth Symphony in E Minor").

The yearning for "going home" is deep and universal. It is a feeling that is larger than the geography of home, often deeper than our actual relationships with anyone there. Even those who have experienced "home" as a very dysfunctional place or community yearn for what the word points to.

The tug to find or return "home" triggers a hope for a network of memory and relationship, sometimes romanticized with time. That network is what the word *community* reaches for. For most of us, those memories of home—its places and people, its notion of "the way things were" and the values that lay beneath that world—remain the mental image of what community is about.

We need to belong—to be part of a larger world. The need to belong drives us to community, a place where we know we belong. It is also a place where we will be safe—a kind of "home base" in the world's chaotic game of "tag." It is a place where you are valued for what you are in yourself, but also a place that often sees more in you than you see in yourself. All of this is wrapped up in the word *community,* and all of it is a mix of people and places, memories and values.

This chapter is about community and our continuing search for it. I base this discussion on three assumptions: (1) that in this society one has fewer and fewer opportunities to find community, (2) that congregations in the past have been important sources of community, and (3) that a major challenge to congregations everywhere is to feed the world's need for community of meaning and relationship. I present this challenge as the fourth we need to address if our congregations are to be as creative in the world of the future as they have been in the past.

"Where is the community I knew as a child?" What a tiresome refrain that has become. Politicians use it to plug their programs; advertisers use it to flog their merchandise. I am suspicious of the nostalgia that circles like a vulture around the concept. I remember the times I grew up in, and I know now how many injustices were a part of that world. My nostalgia blots out things I'd rather not remember—such as living on the "right" or "wrong" side of the tracks, the systemic devaluation of women and girls, the inability to cope with ethnic diversity, the economy that favored me at the expense of many others, the racial phobias we breathed.

Right from the start we need to remind ourselves of the mixed character of our memory and the ambiguous images to which it may lead us.

But John Gardner gives reasons why "community" is a bedrock of society:

Families and communities are the ground-level generators and preservers of values and ethical systems. No society can remain vital or even survive without a reasonable base of shared values—and such values are not established by edict from the lofty levels of the society. They are generated chiefly in the family, school, and other intimate settings in which people deal with one another face to face. The ideals of justice and compassion are nurtured in communities.

Where community exists it confers upon its members identity, a sense of belonging, a measure of security. Individuals acquire a sense of self partly from their continuous relationships to others, and from the culture of their native place....

A community has the power to motivate its members to exceptional performance. It can set standards of expectation for the individual and provide the climate in which great things happen.[1]

John Gardner's contention, and mine, is that whatever faults that traditional form of community had, as a "web of interdependency and mutual obligation" it was a powerful influence in our society. It had a central generative force in shaping our personal lives and our sense of self-esteem; it had impact upon our understanding of the role of families; it influenced the values we sought to live by and shaped many of the structures in which we live.

There may be no consensus on exactly what *community* means. My use of the "going home" image indicates how each of us in our different experiences of home has a deep but unique perspective on what community means. Each of us has had experiences in which that "web of interdependence" was truly there for us—perhaps in our families of origin, in a sports team or a school group in which we felt alive and connected. For some of us it may have been a situation in which we, with others, experienced pressure, opposition, challenge, or even persecution; for others it may have been moments of group engagement in a task. The experiences of the web of community may have been the pain of exclusion from another community—looking over the wall, as it were, to a joy that was denied us.

Many of us have found powerful experiences of genuine community in our congregations, or in some group associated with our churches. Tragically, many of us have also been in congregations in which we had to look over the walls of exclusion to see community that others experienced but to which we were outsiders.

Wherever we have found it, community leaves its mark upon us. Evidence is accumulating that people deprived of a sense of community in early years carry deprivation through life. Evidence also indicates that where the framework of nurturing community has been violated and become abusive, victims often perpetuate similarly abusive relationships in future generations.

Community is much more than something for which we have nostalgia. It is clear that it is a matter of life and death. Because it is so important, we have tended to seek community in many places in recent history. And in most places where we used to find it, it seems in increasingly short supply. That may be why we feel so nostalgic about it!

Losses of Community

The Idea of Neighborhood

Right after World War II a national obsession with finding community fueled middle-class America's migration to the suburbs.2 The move to the suburbs—to the expanding Levittowns of America—was a search not only for a house and a plot of ground, but also for the myth of close-knit human community, a place where one could belong. What these seekers found rarely matched their romantic image of community. They found that houses in suburbia can feel as isolating as apartments in a city; suburban people were busy and hard to get to know beyond superficiality. They found that communication with neighbors was impeded by the roar of lawnmowers. They found charcoal smoke and commuter traffic but not always a sense of community.

Today neighborhoods continue to be thought of as sources of community, but fewer and fewer actually deliver the goods in the city or in the suburb. *Neighbor* is often the new word for *stranger*.

Today's migrations take several forms. From the suburbs many are moving to the bucolic outlands of exurbia or small towns, any place on the current list of the "fifty best places to live." But there they are rapidly re-creating what they don't like about suburbia. Many nonwhite middle-class populations are repeating the white suburban migration of the fifties and sixties, with about as much hope in discovering community. (Their churches are moving from inner cities to the suburbs, following the example of mainline denominations. Those that have stayed in the inner city provide genuine hope for community,3 but they need to pay attention to the problem mainline churches have had, preserving the vitality of their church communities when many members move to suburbia.) Then some of the migration has reversed itself back to the city, where it is hoped that new structures of community can be built. The operative word is *hope*.

Recent migrants to the more affluent suburbs live in isolation from one another within developments walled off from the outside world and protected by armed guards. These wealthy ghettos may well be safer than the urban ghetto, but the jury is out as to whether they actually provide the life-giving qualities that result in a deep sense of grounding and belonging. Does community really live there?

Finding a sense of life-giving community in one's neighborhood has proven to be a search for a will-o'-the-wisp as the twentieth century moves into the twenty-first.

The Idea of Community in the Work Place

Within American society, many others have traditionally found their basic community in the work place. For generations many corporations and businesses nurtured the sense of the work place as more than just a place to make a living. Such businesses genuinely fostered loyalty; mutual caring coexisted with annual profit. At times worker loyalty to the company led both worker and company to make significant sacrifices for that relationship.

No more. *The Downsizing of America* is the title of a recent book, but it is also an apt description of an experience many employees are discovering in the companies for which they work and to which they have had life-long loyalties.4 People used to laugh about the meaning of IBM, saying it meant "I've Been Moved." But in some sense it was proud laughter—proud of the commitment of the company to its employees, a company that was willing to invest in them, willing to strengthen their careers and the company at the same time. There is not much laughter at IBM since the massive layoffs of the eighties and nineties. *The Downsizing of America* points to town after town, company after company where the workers are experiencing downsizing as a shocking betrayal—all the more shocking because of their assumptions about the company as a place of community. They thought they belonged!

Particularly poignant are stories of families that have committed themselves for several generations to an employer considered to be almost "family"—at least until the downsizing started. One such story about AT&T ends: "The corporation of my parents did, after all, pay for my education and help me become a successful adult. At times, I wish I could stay in the secure arms of Ma Bell, but she no longer exists."[5]

Discussing this corporate phenomenon, *The Downsizing of America* points to the erosion of a sense of community that goes beyond the individual to the fabric of the town itself. The sense of community in the town erodes as its taxpayers and volunteers have their lives and incomes disrupted. It is increasingly difficult to find community in the work place.

Many who did not find community with their employers came to rely upon labor unions as a rich and real community. The refrain of the old labor song "Solidarity Forever" says, "We shall not be, we shall not be moved!" What a statement of community commitment to one another.

But from their strong, central role in the work life of large parts of the population in the thirties, forties, and fifties, labor unions have declined sharply in number and in influence. Part of this is no doubt due to the changing face of the American economy, shifting as it has from manufacturing to the service sector (in which labor can sometimes be more easily exploited, but in which workers do not seem as ready to join unions). Fewer and fewer people turn to unions and their union halls as sources of community.

The Idea of Group Activities

Other realms of living express losses of community. Many activities that formerly gathered enthusiastic groups of people who knew one another and acted together for the fun of it have become professionalized and distanced from ordinary citizens. Sports, music, theater, and the arts were once home-made activities engaging the creativity of all sorts of people. There was spontaneous group singing around a piano, guitar, or accordion. There were high school teams and pick-up sand-lot games. Perhaps the only remainder of this from the past is the urban neighborhood basketball scrimmages today. Almost all have become spectator activities.

Even though spectator sports are once-removed from personal participation, they still build a kind of community such as that known by diehard Red Sox fans.[6] But even this residue of community seems to be eroding. The *New York Times* describes the phenomenon in a headline: "Owners' New Strategy: Take the Team and Run."[7] Fans, for whom the team has become an icon of their city and a focus of their sense of community, are forced to go to court to try to keep owners from chasing dollars to another town.

This sense of a loss of community seems to be pervasive. The theme and image of a Harvard professor's January 1995 essay titled "Bowling Alone: America's Declining Social Capital"[8] was picked up by countless columnists, speechmakers, and preachers as a cogent statement of the American predicament. Robert Putnam's image was a simple one: that America had until recently been a nation of bowling leagues, where thousands regularly gathered with teammates in bowling alleys to take on another team in an evening of beer and pretzels, pizza and laughter. Putnam's research had led him to an unsettling discovery—"more Americans are bowling today than ever before, but bowling in organized leagues has plummeted in the last decade or so."[9] People, Putnam suggested, are taking a communal activity and making of it a profoundly private experience. People, he concluded, are bowling alone.

The dramatic simplicity of Putnam's point probably was what led to the quick spread of his idea, which appeared even in President Clinton's speeches. The truth is much more complex, of course, than the sound byte "bowling alone." Putnam put his argument in a context of many other phenomena of society in which there *are* increased personal commitments to group concerns.[10] And yet the overall impression that emerges from his analysis is that in spite of some positive movements toward community (environmental groups, for example) there is trouble in River City in terms of community values. William Raspberry, the distinguished columnist of the *Washington Post,* succinctly calls it "our crisis of community."[11]

More than a decade ago, Robert Bellah and his colleagues[12] documented what they saw to be a shifting of ground in American society away from commitment and community to a more raw individualism and an individual pursuit of happiness. Although their analysis was of a limited sector of the public, the book became a bestseller among a wide group of people who seem to have identified Bellah's thesis as something they recognized in their world.

Bellah's hope is for "social transformation," a theme consistent with John Gardner's passion for the rebirth of community within society. There is little specific direction for those who seek to build community for the future. The problem may lie deeper than these analyses, in the very way we have structured our social relations.[13]

Again, my thesis in this chapter is that the church of the future must become a center within society that feeds and supports the human need for community. The challenge is made more important because of the increasing experience of deprivation of community. The challenge is made more difficult because of the church's loss of credibility as a source of community in our time.

The Church: Its Role, Past and Present

Historically Americans have looked to our churches for community. Realizing the erosion of a sense of community in modern congregations, one reads almost with astonishment of the powerful community in congregations of just a few generations ago. Extraordinary immigrant congregations supported people from "the old country" while they were finding their bearings in a strange continent. Even today new generations of immigrants discover the life-giving power of faith-communities critical to their assimilation into the society. Powerful faith communities among slaves in the eighteenth and nineteenth centuries brought spiritual growth and personal strength in the midst of dehumanizing conditions. Congregations formed on the frontiers strengthened the generations that built a nation. Congregations in our cities challenged the powers that be, the builders of towns and industries. Congregations built colleges and universities and invented forms of social service to the poor and neglected. Congregations provided a support system for families, the locus in which most people found their most critical expression of community. Congregations were centers of education before public education was invented. While these religious communities were doing all that, they went about their more routine but perhaps more important functions— giving people a challenging place to belong, a place that stood by, witnessing to large purposes and a call to serve others. They generated people who built the structures of society.

More than that, and closer to home—I expect that any reader of this book has felt the power of community in a congregation. There are moments like the one described by Isaiah—when he saw God in the temple and discovered his life's vocation—moments when ordinary people find themselves powerfully moved by the Spirit to reevaluate their lives and families and vocations. (Such moments sometimes occur when the person sitting next to them in the pew is thinking, *What an ordinary Sunday service this is!*) Whole congregations have discovered themselves to be a people, a community, in biblical stories of the people of God. Many people have there heard a new call to themselves or to their world and have begun to respond to it. There are moments when a person's intense sense of lostness and isolation is broken through in ordinary things like making music with a choir. Or even hearing music being made by others. There are times when broken relationships are healed in congregations—God knows how! There are congregations—you and I could name some of them—where, among quite ordinary folk, some are inspired to become quite extraordinary, to see the thing that needs doing, the word that needs saying, the hurt that needs sharing. There are thousands of congregations—obsolete though the experts think them to be—where people simply find the strength to keep on keeping on. There are minds wandering through the innumerable words of a tired, retreaded sermon that are suddenly electrified by a phrase, a note, a hint in which the Word appears with conviction and power, frequently without the knowledge of the preacher. There are individual lives and ordinary families fed and sustained in acts of worship or of being together. This is the stuff of congregational life. The power of community is born again in us and around us.

That has always been one of the functions of congregations.

You see, most of the stories of life-changing community are distinctly anonymous; they occur without fanfare. Britton Johnston and Sally Johnson participated in a four-year effort by congregations in the Midwest that wanted to reach out beyond their parish bounds with their sense of community. The authors tell scores of stories, many of them of only a page or less, each describing the impact of these "nonheadline" moments in which community comes alive.[14]

The fact is, however, that congregations today are rarely seen as centers of genuine community. Catholic theologian John Linnan says very directly that congregations are obsolete as centers of human support and growth.[15] His comment reflects the feeling of many. The extraordinary power of community that congregations of the past have shown and that we have experienced from time to time is not very evident in our world. The congregations that "outsiders" see do not seem to express the presence of the kind of community that those people are hungry for.

For all too many, congregations appear to be self-satisfied conglomerations of like-minded people. Non-Christians often use the word *hypocritical* to describe what they see in congregations. A Midwest conference of the United Methodist Church did a courageous piece of work in focus groups asking nonchurched people to describe the public perception of the church.[16] Almost no comments indicated an attraction to churches because of the sense of community found there. Instead people said: "I have yet to find a church where people want to be there because of shared values instead of just being cliquish and judgmental."

People of our time, whose common value is sometimes "what's in it for me?" have a hard time seeing congregations as the source of genuine community.

Reginald Bibby, a sociologist who has studied churches across Canada and their relationship to the public, documents the way people in Canada seem to be looking for the benefits—including a sense of community—that the church has traditionally tried to provide. He points out two things he learned: that people are not looking for the church and that the churches are not looking for people but focus instead on their institutional survival.[17] Hoge, Johnson, and Luidens make a similar point in their study of unchurched Presbyterians.[18]

People are finding less and less sense of community in their world; they seem to be looking for it, but one of the very institutions that has traditionally met the need for community (and still does for many) simply is not on the radar screen of many who really want community. People simply do not look to the churches for that which is supposed to be one of its great values.

That is why I see this as a major challenge for the church: (1) to discover how to be and to support authentic community and (2) to see that those hungry for community in our society can find it. Being such a community is itself a tremendous challenge, but the more daunting task is to change the perceptions of people who have come to think of the church's expression of community in terms of hypocrisy. Neither part of the dual challenge will be easy.

We must begin where we are. The church of tomorrow will evolve from the churches we have. The challenge to develop authentic community is a challenge to each congregation, building on whatever community is already in place.

We begin with enormous handicaps. Our society has lost many traditionally strong sources of community, giving rise to an isolating form of individualism. Congregations, one of the sources of community in previous generations, are themselves beset by the same demons that inhabit our society. Their own resources for "being community" even for members are severely eroded. And, more tragically, congregations have lost public credibility as potential sources of community.

Where do we begin?

I will first identify three modes for approaching both the tasks noted above (being community and helping people connect with it). Then I want to note some strategies by which we can move out from where we are.

Three Modes of Being and Generating Community

Congregations as Community

Analysts of congregations rightly point out that different cultural situations have different needs and possibilities for being community. Urban, suburban, and rural settings all call for different kinds of congregational life that in itself provides the community people need.

In some rural situations congregations can still offer the kind of experience of community that embraces almost all of life. Work life, family life, public and private life—all are lived out in such a way that Sunday worship does reflect a unified world. There all the congregation's children go to the same schools and everyone goes to the same movies. There congregations can still be a focus in which the whole life of the whole neighborhood is celebrated and offered to God in the community of faith. Fewer and fewer of our rural locations reflect this almost romantic view of what rural communities may have been a century ago. Even in the most rural of areas today television brings fragmented values and the presence of a whole outside world that dissipates the sense of togetherness with one's neighbors. Consolidation of schools may mean that the community children are spread out in schools located in several counties.

A few urban congregations also have some of the feel of rural congregations—a sense of being an enclave in which the whole of life is
shared. This is particularly true for ethnic groups, but it is also true for
small congregations of Episcopalians or Presbyterians, Baptists or United
Methodists who have maintained their historical presence in urban locations.

In many urban, metropolitan, and suburban congregations, the
ability to be community as a single entity is severely circumscribed.
Moments of community in great occasions of worship can be nurturing
and dramatic. I have known great pastors who, by preaching and leading
worship, bring the gift of community to incredibly diverse groups.
Indeed, the great preachers of the nineteenth and early twentieth century
built real community through preaching. Dr. George Docherty, retired
pastor of New York Avenue Presbyterian Church in Washington, D.C.,
used the Sunday morning service announcement period to bring people
into community with one another. Community can also be achieved as a
group cooperates in great mission tasks or even—God help us—building
projects! For the most part, however, urban congregations have to seek
ways in which subsets of the whole congregation can find community
and also ways in which the congregation can support the development of
human community in the larger society.

As our nation embraces diversity, congregations of people with the
same background are likely to be essential "home bases" for people
overwhelmed by strange language and cultural values. Such congregations retain a role they have played for centuries as new Americans have
sought sometimes to integrate themselves into this new world, and at
other times to maintain an identity. Our challenge will be to help those
who depend on this sense of community move into the wider society.
Will ethnic congregations remain as isolating islands radically separated
from society, or will they become places of safety encouraging and faci-
litating engagement with the wider culture? Will the remnant congregations retain their identity until the last member dies? The churches themselves will need to struggle with this question: At what point—if ever—
does a community of "apartness" begin to be at war with the community
in Christ?

All congregations must explore what it means to be a congregation
within a particular heritage and faith story—honoring both the large faith
story and also the local flavor of that particular place and people. The

genuine community they have to offer society is not a simple togetherness, but a being-together out of commitment, a common story, and
shared values. It is a working out of the meaning of the biblical story—
that we are brothers and sisters of one another, children of a purposeful
God. Community is not just a nice product we have to sell to society; it is
what we are as Christians. To the extent that we have forgotten that, we
must rediscover the biblical grounds of our being in community and articulate that larger sense of community in a way that leaves space for the
necessary "safe places" many of us need in order to deal with diversity
and change in our lives.

Congregations as Generators of Community

The extent to which a congregation can or should actually "be community," as described above, differs depending on its setting. But wherever
it is, a congregation has a function of being a generator of community—
an institution that seeks by what it does to stimulate opportunities for
people to find community with others. Let me name a few ways that
congregations are already working to make that happen, both within their
own structures and also within the society outside the congregation's
bounds.

The image of the house church comes to mind first. In widely dis-
parate forms house churches have been around forever. (Many of the
congregations described in the New Testament were probably house
churches.) Basically house churches are an attempt to do all that a "standard model parish" does without the focus on buildings, staffs, and budgets that other congregations find so confining. Characteristically a group
of families covenant together to become a church, and they build the
structures and patterns of life they need. House churches often fulfill a
need for intimacy and closeness that ordinary congregations cannot sustain. They permit a clarity of life that other congregations trying to meet
requirements of the institutional church seem to get distracted from. Such
churches sometimes are "stand alone" entities. Others understand themselves to be special "subdivisions" of the parent congregations.

A house church often begins from an impulse to find more authentic
community, a more authentic sense of church. This need must be af-
firmed and supported. Many congregations see the establishment of a

house church as a threat—loss of members and loss of pledges! That may be true. Yet local congregations need to have a deeper understanding of their task. The task of generating community includes listening for times to start house churches. A less well understood fact is that most house churches have a limited life-span; in our society they rarely become permanent institutions. This means that congregations need to be ready to help the people who are called to launch house churches, but they need also to stand by to give support when it is time for the house church to die. Without such help, the death of a house church is a long-drawn-out experience with a deep, painful sense of failure. With real help, such a death often leads to a resurrection of faith and vocation in the congregation and for the former members of the house church.

Congregations need to understand the rich opportunity for generating community that already exists in ordinary congregational groups. Established groups, such as Sunday school classes, choirs, teachers groups, guilds, even committees, can get so focused on their assignment that they simply overlook the chance to help generate genuine community (in spite of voluminous research showing that most tasks are performed best if the participants have a sense of community and caring with their fellow-workers). Every congregation has such groups. Some care for the altar; some arrange the music or perform it; some attend or teach weekly classes; some make sandwiches for the hungry; some plan how to change local politics; some take care of the church garden. Each of these ongoing groups is full of people yearning for the experience of community; each of these groups has the potential to become more of a community than it is. Somebody in each congregation and in each group needs to be aware of the potential for community available within the group. Part of the church's task is to recognize these opportunities to generate community in the ordinary interactions that make up congregational life.

Across the denominational spectrum I find people increasingly trying to find out how the church board—long the home of interminable meetings and grinding debate—can become one of those places in which community happens. Church boards have a special calling to transform themselves from places noted for slogging, depressing work to places of community and spiritual growth. Charles Olsen has provided us with insights and resources for helping a congregation do just that. He wants boards to undertake what he calls "worshipful work."[19]

The term *small groups* covers a wide range of efforts to generate community within congregations. As I look back over my life, I see that I spiritually and personally grew most when I was involved in a small personal group, experiencing intense community and building relationships that have fed me through the years since the group came to an end. The groups varied widely: a two-year group of ten (five seminary couples infatuated with personal therapy and trying to understand marriage); a six-year group of seven to ten (couples and single parents in a parish); a five-year group of eight long-in-the-tooth clergymen; a two-year group of three men trying to learn to pray together.... So what I have to say here is based on a personal witness to the power one can experience in such small groups, however they are organized and run.

Local congregations need to be in the business of generating small-group opportunities for their people—small groups tasked with no specific purpose other than "being community" with one another within the context of faith. Experts suggest different strategies, courses of study, methods of managing the groups, of supervising or not supervising leaders. I have found many of their insights helpful, but I get nervous about experts who approach small groups ideologically, as the only way to be church. Yes, I know how much I have gained in small groups. But I also know that there have been seasons in my life when small groups "did not fit." And I do not believe congregations need to be in the business of "cookie-cutting" everybody into small groups. Generating small groups and helping them to nurture—that is the task, not coercing people into small groups. If the congregation does not work hard at generating small groups, they probably won't happen. If the congregation gets high and mighty about them, they can generate an explosive reaction. That's the tension. We must face the tension and move ahead. If you are pushing too hard, you'll soon find out.

The world of small-group advocates includes at least three different types of small-group development, each with its true believers.

The Asian model assumes a small group exists for the purpose of expanding the church's membership and expanding lay leadership. Such use of small groups has been part of the explosive growth of Korean churches. In this model a church automatically assigns each new "walk-in" member to a small group Most new members are brought in by the small groups themselves, each of which "splits" when it reaches a certain size. The theory is that church members cannot genuinely "belong" if they are not in a face-to-face group for spiritual nurture and growth. As adapted in America, this model is also seen as a primary way to lead laypeople into full ministries as apostles of the church. Here in the States I have seen this model work in a few places—primarily in new church starts. It is problematic in long-standing congregations where "small groups" is brought in by a pastor or leadership group in spite of significant opposition from church members. In American churches this model also runs into problems in that groups do not, on the whole, seem able to "split." Indeed, small groups have a hard time being able to assimilate new members easily. In this culture, groups seem to become effective in pastoral care of group members rather than in church extension. Churches that start small groups hoping for membership growth often find not membership growth but a quality of caring and nurturing that has enormous impact upon the spiritual growth of group members and their families.

A second small-group model is from the tradition of human relations training; the interpersonal power of these small-group experiences has revolutionized many lives. At one time characterized as "sensitivity training," these groups have become standard fare in helping managers learn how to work with other people. These face-to-face groups encourage authentic communication and the direct facing of human dynamics that get hidden in ordinary discourse. They encourage people to "tell it like it is." These small groups can be deeply introspective and long-lasting, becoming a primary focal point of members' lives. Children of the "T-Group" experiences of the fifties and sixties, these groups find it difficult to incorporate new members or to let old members move on when they need to. Many of these groups include an explicit or a tacit concern to help members build more healthful personal and interpersonal relationships. They help people get clear and direct feedback on their behavior. As a source of personal growth, these groups may be unmatched, but I have known plenty to bomb out.

The third small-group model is based on South American Catholic lay groups called "base communities." which have become centers of powerful movements for liberation, both in politics and the church. They center in biblical study and engage with the important issues of people's lives and communities. Primarily lay-led, they have spread across South America wherever the Catholic church is found. In North America the attempt to generate base communities has not been as contagious as in South America. Here, even Catholic congregations considered to be centers of base community work rarely claim more than a modest membership participation. Within the Catholic Church in the U. S., these groups are known as Small Faith Communities. (The acronym SFC appears frequently in Catholic conference advertisements.) The energy the South American base community movement finds in South America may well come from that particular cultural situation; until the past two generations, Catholics in South America had no access to the Bible in the vernacular. The energy of base community life may be analogous to the experience of laity in Northern Europe in the sixteenth century when they first had access to scriptures in common languages.

The point is not that all the models have flaws, but that all the models provide very practical ways for the churches to be generators of community. If these models are not adequate, we should be about developing better ones.

Churches have much to offer as generators of community in a society that is increasingly deprived of "community." Members of congregations have a right to call upon the church to help them connect with community.

Congregations as Support for Community

The ability of a congregation to *be* community depends on the world in which it exists. But even in places where the congregation has a limited ability to be community, as may be the case in large metropolitan areas, it can still have a strong role *generating* community. Here, I want to address the challenging role of the congregation in *supporting* community within society—another important dimension of its calling in today's world.

Despite the breakdown in family life deplored by society's leaders, it is clear that most peoples' primary experience of community occurs within the family. More and more people experience that community in diverse family systems—single-parent families, groups of singles living as families, empty-nest families, and extended families. Statistics on the increased number of single-parent families, of traditional families without children, of nonmarried people as family units—all continue to point to the changing character of what we call "family" and its impact upon our society.

And it is in families that most ordinary people find that sense of closeness that fosters the growth of identity. Most people go to "family" when hurt or damaged by life experience. And, for many people, "family" is where they can count on being taken in, no matter what.

Even the enormous potential for abuse and manipulation in no way detracts from the life-giving potential of family life.

The congregation is one of the few family back-up systems in our society. *Simply being there* at the critical events that make and shape families is a central function of congregations—the bonding of two people,[20] the birth or adoption of children, the milestones in children's lives, celebrations of new stages of life or work, the trauma of illness, the encounters with guilt, depression or despair, the uncertainties of new challenges, the farewells of death. Most of the churches have liturgies and traditions that help to bring many of these transitions and crises into perspective with a creative and redemptive sense of purpose modeled in our credal statements.

I sense that, over the generations, the churches have allowed their participation in these events to become routine performances. I am impressed with the way many of those same churches are struggling to bring those life-transition ministries back to life. Perhaps the most visible of those struggles has been in the churches that practice infant baptism. Only half a century ago, baptisms were routinely private affairs to which parents and close friends gathered with a pastor engaged to "do" the child. That still happens in some places, but more often baptism is a major public affirmation of identity in community. Marriage itself is being renewed as a rite as a result of many forms of marriage enrichment available through congregations. Family crises—including those we have ignored in the past (retirement, divorce)—need to be explored as ways to undergird the strength and health of the family. The debate about "marriage" of same-sex couples may be beneficial to the churches if it leads to affirmation of the larger purposes of and need for human community and gets beyond matters of genital behavior.

Congregations have another function in supporting the experience of community in our society. They need to encourage people to look beyond their own personal life or even family life. Congregations produce the people who commit themselves to the public—who work on community boards, who help the schools, who volunteer where society needs assistance. Congregations also support community by challenging people to generosity and to become philanthropists outside their own family and congregational life.[21]

The Dilemma, the Challenge, Some Beginning Clues

We begin with a difficult dilemma: Our society has lost many of the ingredients that made for community even as a new individualism has appeared that divides and separates. Congregations, caught up in their own survival and enculturated in the larger societal trends, have lost much of their ability to be community, to generate community for their people, or even, in some cases, to support community. All too often our congregations have become another part of the problem—just one more organization competing for the attention of people, hawking its wares as superior to those of others, and, in effect, further fragmenting whatever experience of community remains. The public all too frequently has recognized us as part of the problem and has increasingly stopped looking to us for answers or help in their search for a sense of community.

The gift of community, so badly needed by society, so longed for, has not been nourished within the church. We have lost touch with it ourselves. It is doubly ironic that we are the people to whom community was especially revealed, whose theology articulates God as God-in-community, and who came onto the world's stage as a people noted for how they loved one another. Who can wonder that the world does not look to us for answers when we have been so prodigal in the waste of our gifts?

In the face of this dilemma, the fourth challenge to the churches is that we must once again become a wellspring of the experience of community within our world. Within a generation or two we must reshape the life of the church so that this world will be shot through with nourishing, provocative community that excludes no one from a sense of belonging. Within that life-span we must also make strides to be that place that is known to side with, encourage, and generate community throughout our society. If we address these imperatives we will be known once more as the place to go to discover what it feels like to be in a community, cared for, forgiven, and—yes—challenged!

In the Beginning

The greatest single resource we have for rebuilding vital community in our congregations is the one that is closest at hand. Who we are and what we are about is the heart of what every congregation does whenever it meets for worship. Who we are is the community of God, the community for others. What we are about is being that community living within the Power from beyond ourselves and witnessing to God's love and forgiveness for all. Every time we gather to worship God, that reality lies all around us. It is there for the taking. It is there to be soaked in, whether we understand it fully or not. In worship we grasp for that which is beyond our comprehension. The act of worship itself is a cry to God for community, but it is also paradoxically an opening through which God's power to give community gets into our lives and into our inadequate community. Worship reaches out for community and is at the same time a means by which that for which we pray comes to us. The opportunity comes so regularly and routinely that we often overlook its power to change us and our congregations.

Worship is our definition of ourselves in relationship to God and our side of a dialogue that is God's definition of us. There is no other one place in which the congregation tries to express itself before God—who it is, what it needs, what it values, what it believes in, what it grieves, what it celebrates. Attention to the quality and content of worship is the central resource for rediscovering our identity and reconnecting to our roots.

I do not mean to say that worship is valuable primarily as a means to develop community, although I admit that it can be used that way to great effect. I do not mean to say that sacraments and ordinances, music and liturgy, preaching and prayer themselves serve primarily to constitute a solid human community, but, again, I admit that they can help do this.

My point is that the central moment for every congregation is its moment of worship. That is where it most defines itself in dynamic relationship to that Power that is the source of its identity. That is where it seeks to draw on the Spirit of that Power to bring new life to the individual and to the community. It is dynamic. Something happens there.

Worship is the place at which the identity of the congregation is dramatically acted out and also discovered in relationship to and in dialogue with God.

Great worship does build community. Great worship opens hearts to hear the cries of loneliness and joy of the congregation. Great worship places us with the great pain of the world and of our neighbors, and it sharpens our commitment to making a difference. Great worship helps us celebrate the grandeur and the misery of existence. Great worship makes and should make great demands upon us—to be committed to serving God's people and God's world. Great worship brings healing where there is illness, strength where there is weakness, forgiveness where there is guilt. It is the doorway through which God tells us who we are and empowers us to be what God calls us to be. It is not something to fool around with or treat lightly.

As we use all the resources at our command to build the community that the world needs, worship remains our central resource.

But What Comes Next?

In pursing community, we must begin by recognizing that there is no one answer to the problems we face. Each congregation starts at a different place; let's agree that no starting place is better than another. It also means that the answers we come up with will be specific to where we are and who we are. Our direction may be different from others. No national program, no ideological commitment to "the correct way" is likely to give us more than some initial direction, some hunches. Indeed, answers will have to be home-grown. Trial and error must become our standard operating system. That, in itself, may be one of the most important clues to moving ahead.

The technologically astute among us call this trial-and-error approach "action research," a method in which action is taken after the best insight is gathered from as wide a spectrum as possible; the results of the action are sifted and evaluated in preparation for the next step. Most church "programs" propose a series of actions that make logical sense, but they don't take into account the fact that the first step never goes the way it is designed. Each step then gets further and further from what was intended. The program ends as a disappointment or disaster that usually is blamed on "the program" or the church agency that sold it to them. I am not talking about something terribly complicated. I'm suggesting we pay attention to what happens every time we try something, then make adjustments. Frankly, that's all most consultants worth their salt help us do—pay attention to what has happened and learn from our experience.

Starting where we are means that we are dealing with slow and incremental change, change that will take years. Let me be honest. I am saying that meeting this and the other challenges I am describing puts us on a course that does not end. It does not "get there"; it will never be done. We are embarking on a journey into God's future. Given this reality, if we are willing to accept it, what then do we do first?

I think the most promising first step is to think about and work on boundaries. In their hearts congregations have a story, an experience with God, a heritage—one that is different from that of the general society. Unfortunately, congregations have become enculturated to the extent that they are unable to differentiate themselves from the society around them. They have "gone native." This has happened gradually, over generations, and continues as society's values and stories and heritage infiltrate our lives and congregations. Through exposure to media we assimilate values from a culture that puts little value on human caring. The models of acceptable behavior that we see in our towns and cities—in private citizens and political leaders—also conflict with what our faith and the scriptures tell us. Behaviors to which our children are exposed are the antithesis to what we want them to learn.

There are congregations that see (and try to practice) a severe disconnection from the outside world as a cure to this enculturation. If our Amish and our fundamentalist brothers and sisters sometimes act in ways we do not understand, it is this distinctive difference they are defending. And celebrating. I do not choose or recommend that way, but I have enormous sympathy for it.[22]

I suggest that we mainline churches rethink the issues of boundary. When the boundary between a congregation and the world outside is so blurred that we can no longer tell the one world from the other, one's identity takes on the coloration of the dominant society. The church then operates by society's standards without reference to its own story, heritage, and values, and the individual has no community compass to determine true directions for life.

We must pay attention to boundaries between the church and the community. That means rethinking what it is that makes us a special community. It means rediscovering and rehearsing the story of where we came from and whose we are. It means reconnecting with the power of our heritage. It means redefining our values in today's world. This is an internal task—one we must do for ourselves and with ourselves. It calls us to become a learning community in brand new ways.

Most churches think of education as being synonymous with Sunday school. That is totally inadequate even to help us relearn our own story.[23] Accepting the challenge of becoming a center of community for tomorrow's world commits us to massive new efforts for adult education about the faith. We need to face the facts: that most of us in the church today have forgotten our story; we maintain our heritage only by habits we learned from those who knew the story by heart. Each generation has to reappropriate the story and connect with the experience of faith. It does not suffice to be able to repeat what parents told us a long time ago. Adults of this generation have remedial work to do before they will be able to communicate the story to their own children and grandchildren. That is what is called for—not just an hour on Sunday mornings.

Our congregations can be wonderful associations of people, but they cannot become the kind of life-giving community we need unless we reinvest ourselves in the story of faith—remembering and experiencing again our slavery in Egypt and our release from captivity, experiencing the power of false gods and of judgment, experiencing the surprise of the appearance of the Promised One, and discovering the power of the Spirit. Second-hand faith is not enough for the kind of community we need.

Rebuilding the boundary of the congregation means building a community of faith within the congregation that knows itself and can differentiate itself from the spirits of this age. It involves the life of the entire body. This is not a step that happens all at once. Rebuilding such a boundary is what I'd call a boot-strap operation, experimentally moving ahead, testing, then adjusting direction and speed. Let me give some specifics.

The act of entering a congregation is an act of leaving one world and set of values and entering another; it is an experience of crossing a boundary. Church leaders need to help people crossing that boundary recognize it as a passage from one kind of life to another. We cannot do that unless we ourselves become more conscious of who we are in this community and how we are different. Again, I see this as "boot-strap change." At this point in history, church members really have forgotten much that makes the church distinctive. That means every entry of every

outsider becomes a double opportunity for building new community: It
provides the congregation with an opportunity to understand itself more
deeply (or to deepen that community). It is also an opportunity to help
the newcomer learn what this community actually stands for and is.

Every entry must dramatize that move from one life to another.
Above I discussed recent changes in baptismal practices. They can be a
useful image of boot-strap change. The initial attempts to change baptismal practices involved a tortuous process of pastors arm wrestling individual families. The first step was to make baptism part of the Sunday
morning public worship. The practice was enriched by a sometimes fur-
tive effort to educate godparents and parents. Eventually the forms of
liturgies began to change, giving congregations a more active part in
baptism. I now go to a parish in which baptismal "classes" are scheduled,
and candidates are prayed for weeks before baptisms, which are important festival events. Clearly, what has happened did not happen all at
once. Indeed, I don't think we knew where it was all going when we
started. We made one step, and then the next followed. Different congregations did it different ways. Who knows what the next steps will be?
But all these signs point to a growing sense of what it means to belong to
this peculiar community, to what it means to cross this boundary. Each
step can lead to the next. Each step starts where people are.

There are other entry points.[24] Every one of them—new membership, transfer from another congregation, confirmation or other affirmation of membership, return from a sabbatical, return after a long journey
or years of living elsewhere—provides opportunities for the boot-strap
process I have described. Anyone crossing the boundary provides an
opportunity to reinforce the meaning of the community to members and
to those entering it.

Increasingly, congregations are adopting more stringent training for
new members, but rare still is the congregation that genuinely owns standards for membership, takes responsibility for modeling those standards,
and is prepared to enforce those standards upon new members. Some ten
or fifteen years ago, my own denomination made a decision (in spite of
all the dangers of top-down decisions, this was so done, but not without
considerable grass-roots agitation!) to make tithing the standard of giving
for the denomination.[25] The national board argued and fought and then
decided to accept tithing as their personal standard and to recommend it
to the parishes. Parish after parish argued about it. Some "accepted" and

did nothing. Others decided it was not for them. Others said no, then a
few years later changed their stance. In time, most members were exposed to the idea that tithing is one expectation of the members of this
particular denomination. The impact on per-member giving has been
most positive; but that is irrelevant to my point about setting standards of
membership. That brief story illustrates a boot-strap operation of identifying what we are and what our standards are. It also points out that
standards should be set by leaders who will live by them.

What actually distinguishes people who are part of your congregation? Or what should distinguish them? Who should be involved in de-
termining that? How can the congregation affirm and support those who
try to live by those standards?

These questions about setting standards can help you get clarity
about what the community wants to stand for. The specific standards are
legion. What should being a member of this congregation mean about
attendance at public worship? What should it mean in terms of relationships to spouses and children? What should it mean about involvement in
the economic and political world surrounding the congregation? What
does it mean about how members relate to their resources?

Having developed standards for being in the congregation, how do
we then help each other to live by those standards? How do we train new
members of the community about the standards? Working on the boundary means working on issues such as these.

Some congregations are beginning such training for new members,
but most "transfers" from other congregations still bypass the training.
Maybe we need a congregational immigration service and training program, one that reflects the values and standards of the congregation. It
should not be primarily the task of the clergy. Such a program would
call for continuous work in the congregation, reviewing and rethinking
(1) what that congregation understands membership of this church to
mean and (2) how an individual demonstrates those behaviors and trains
for them.

I have described a process of developing community by delineating
the boundary one must cross to enter the community. We begin with
what's left of an identity that may have been distinctive several centuries
ago but which has become overwhelmed by the identity of the social environment. Genuine community in the church can come only with a new
clarity about identity with the Christian faith and a willingness to make
that identity central to the congregation.

Every human crisis point is an opportunity for the congregation to rediscover itself and for the person in crisis to experience a deeper dimension of faith-identity in that community. Ministries to one another in those crises give new and concrete meaning to our identity as a community of faith.

I have already noted the potential of the many groups in every congregation to become centers of life-giving community. Applying bootstrap action-research methods can also help them achieve more of their potential. Beginning where it is, each group can revise its own life in relationship to the deepening sense of identity that the congregation has, and each group can contribute to that identity. Similarly, the congregation that encourages house churches and small-group life will find that those laboratories of community will be able to receive and give much to the congregation's growing sense of identity.

The fourth challenge for the church to face and overcome in the next few generations is to become the place that feeds the world's need for community.

CHAPTER 5

CHALLENGE 5:
To Become an Apostolic People

The church we live in understands "the mission of the church" in very institutional ways. Who is "sent" and where they are sent is a function of decisions made by executives in mission agencies or denominational headquarters. The purposes and priorities of mission are outgrowths of the life of the congregations, judicatories, and groups that make up the church.

The apostolic task (the "sending" or "being sent" function of the church) is managed and directed by the institutional framework of the church. The various denominations have managed this apostolic function in different ways. Most are very serious about it, put major energy into it, work hard to build support for it, and do it as well as they possibly can. It is important to them. Because of the way those systems are structured, however, the focus is on the mission of the *church* (understood, at best, as the universal church, but often as the mission of this particular church or denomination). The central apostolic task of the church is determined by the clergy and the hierarchies, and the laity is relegated to the role of "supporter" of the apostolic work.

As its fifth challenge the church of the future must become fully apostolic. It must be an apostolic people, not an apostolic institution or hierarchy. And each member of the church must see him- or herself as *being* an apostle. You have probably heard this message before, but I say there is much more to it than we have been willing to admit or face.

How Is an "Apostolic People" Different from an "Apostolic Church"?

From the earliest days, the church's common assumption has been that its central business is to go, to be sent, to make disciples across the world. That consciousness of "being sent" has undergirded the church's sense of who and what it is, and it has defined its mission. The early life of the church was consumed by a sense of mission—of reaching out, of crossing boundaries, and of protecting itself against attacks from inside or outside.[1] To be involved in the church's mission was to be sent, to be apostolic.

Two themes dominated Jesus' message to his followers about that mission: (1) that every follower of Jesus was called to reach out as a caring servant of others, like Jesus himself; and (2) that the church itself was to be a community that expanded to the ends of the earth, bringing all manner of people into its life and embrace; the church was to encompass the world.

The concept of mission as understood by the churches of our generation has focused on the second of these themes and consequently the churches organized to accomplish it. The churches honor the first role (the servant role) as genuine and celebrate it in those individual people who live out humble service, but they have shaped their institutional priorities and structures to accomplish the expansionist model. We love Saint Francis, but we organize like Franciscans.

Our self-understanding as Christians is derived from the "Great Commission" that we should make disciples of all the nations, baptizing them in the name of the Father, the Son, and the Holy Ghost.[2] That concept of mission, however, picked up all sorts of cultural accretions as it made its way through the centuries and civilizations through which it passed on its way to us. We did not receive a pristine concept of mission directly from the New Testament; we received an idea of mission as modified by the experiences of the church over the ages. In particular, the concept of mission that dominated the thinking of the late nineteenth-century and early twentieth-century church was heavily shaped by intellectual, economic, and political currents in Western Europe and North America during those same years, years of unprecedented ferment and cultural change.

Enlightenment currents flourished in the universities in which theologians were trained. Assumptions about the superiority of Western culture infected Christians' way of looking at civilizations in which Christianity was not the norm. Missionary thinking was modified by Western cultural elitism. People of other cultures were stereotyped as the poor, ignorant heathen or romanticized as the noble savage. In either case they were defined by Western sensibilities that rarely looked to the flesh and blood lives that were touched.[3]

Economic and political movements led European and North American nations to develop colonial empires in which they took great pride and from which they sometimes took profit. Expeditionary forces went to bring those pagan lands under the protection of the "crown," as some put it. (Americans tipped a hand to God and called it Manifest Destiny.) Patriotism and economics got mixed up with a sense of moral superiority and a deep-felt sense of a call to mission. Different actors represented different mixes of these complex motives.

This theme of mission as the extension of the bounds of Christendom carried the day within the church. In church circles, the word *mission* came to mean the expansion of the church to new lands and to new peoples. Honest enthusiasm for mission merged with national passions for colonial expansion. Supported as it was by cultural, political, economic, and intellectual consensus, the word *mission* became the religious side of the word *imperialism.*

In making this overly simplistic comment, I do not at all question the integrity of the impulse to mission concern that was genuine among leaders of the churches and ordinary members themselves. Some of those leaders were heroic and self-giving by any standard. There was a genuine desire to follow the great commandment of Jesus to "make disciples of all nations." But the cultural milieu in which the people sought to carry out that commandment modified how they understood mission and how they thought it should be done. Culture put a pressure behind the deeply religious convictions of mission-minded Christians.

Those understandings of mission—powerfully religious yet also greatly influenced by cultural images of Christian/Western superiority—shaped our understanding of the roles of church leadership and the design of our institutional forms.

The result was a "top-down" relationship between roles in the church and a "top-down" set of institutional arrangements for doing mission. Those arrangements continue to rule our organization for mission. The

authentication of mission came to be related to validation by the higher
authorities in the churches. Ministry was seen as being valid only if it
was authenticated by those validated by the structural arrangements of
the denominations. Hence the endless debates in the nineteenth and
twentieth centuries in which ecclesiologists and theologians tried to
define whose clergy had validity and whose did not.[4] Those conversations echo through many contemporary negotiations between denominations seeking grounds for reunion.

I'm aware of two ways we validate orders today: through the "franchise" system and the "trickle-down" system.

The franchise system authenticates clergy, ministry, and mission
with the authority of their denominational system. Everyone authenticated in the Presbyterian or United Methodist systems, for example, may
"deliver the goods"—at least to those in that system. They may not cross
over to one of the other systems unless they are authenticated by it. Why
do I use the word franchise? Think in terms of McDonald's. Anywhere
you see the golden arches, you know you will get a McDonald's ham-
burger, not cotton candy. The manager has the franchise, and he or she
has been checked out by the organization. Go in there, the system says,
and you'll get the genuine article. In a church, if the system has the
franchise, you're hooked up to a valid missionary and ministry enterprise. The company stands behind it.

The trickle-down system assumes that validity of ministry comes
from knowledge. So we get brilliant people to cluster in our seminaries
to teach ordination candidates. Those brilliant people pass on all they can
to their students, who are no intellectual slouches themselves. Those
students are expected to pick up "enough" of the professors' knowledge
to preach well enough to pass on sufficient knowledge to the person in
the pew; parishioners thereby become knowledgeable enough to have a
valid lay ministry. Each level loses a bit in prestige, but its purpose is to
channel "enough" to the "lower" levels.

Just what constitutes "enough knowledge" is the subject of considerable debate. Heated arguments occur when people try to define the
enoughs. Although denominations have invested enormous energy and
resources in systems to ensure that enough trickles down, some early
evidence suggests that this may not be happening. The system is not
producing enough theological acumen at the lower levels.[5]

These two caricatures of the churches' authentication systems have this in common: Both assume that ministry is to be authenticated through the organizational system. Validation is passed "down" from those who have a level of knowledge or authority higher than those who are "lower" in the system. To put it in terms used earlier in this book, these systems are intrinsically clericalist. The power to determine authenticity of mission, the power to transmit authenticity or even define it, is reserved to the clergy, whether presbyterial, congregational, or episcopal.

The ordinary member of the church is therefore relegated to the role of "client of the clergy"—the one to be trained in mission, convinced of the clerical definition of ministry, measured by the clergy's standards. And the mission itself is defined and structured by the institution itself.

I trust my stating it this way shows how we, in our domestic ecclesiological life, play out the same game that has been played in our foreign missions approach for generations.[6] In our domestic churches the laity is treated like the overseas clients of the home church's missionary effort; the laity is the pagan, treated as a stranger to the gospel, ignorant of revelation of God, untutored in the ways deemed essential for valid faith and mission. We assume that little or nothing is genuinely of God in the experience of the laity at home or the pagan in far-off countries; God has to be imported into their lives before they can be called into active mission. In this framework the apostolic dimension of the church is obviously located in its clergy and ecclesiatical governors.

I think it is time to say that this tack is bankrupt. Wrong.

The Mission Belongs to God

My basic assumption is that the mission that counts is God's mission, not the church's.[7] That assumption makes us look at the world and *mission* in a new light. We no longer look at the world for the *gaps,* so that we, in mission, can take God to where God is not now. Instead, we look at the world as the arena in which God's care and love are already, everywhere, at work. We do not take mission out; we go out to meet the mission already there. We look for the places to which we are called to take our place in that larger, ongoing mission.

As things are now, we church people look across the world and see the church's congregations, colleges, institutions, and there we see the mission of the church. We take pride in remarkable institutional accomplishments and heroic actions for the faith.

But if with the eyes of faith we look across the very same world, we can see a much larger mission. We can see the loving, judging, life-giving concern of God for the whole of the created order, a concern that calls all of creation into life and into life-giving partnerships. We can view the mission of God as far greater than the mission of our institutions. In God's mission the church has a role, as does each of us. In such a view, many who are not of the church are part of God's mission. Many of them already show great gifts of the Spirit. In such a view of mission, the primary missionaries may be those who can claim no "valid" credentials at all. Many may not be of the household of faith. As God freed the exiles in Babylon through the agency of Cyrus—not one of the people of Israel—so God's distinct mission today is not necessarily solely directed through the church, no matter how much church people defensively claim that place in the scheme of things.[8]

In our time one can see evidence of the mission of God around the world, in movements with which the church has ambivalent relations.[9] I briefly discuss three of the movements in which I see marks of God's mission.

Freedom Movements

Sweeping changes have occurred as oppressed and colonized people have struggled to freedom from political and social bondage. Much of this I see as an expression of a power greater than ours, greater than organizations. In the power of these different movements, I see God reaching out in mission. These movements have swept across colonial nations, particularly in Africa, East Asia, and Central Asia. They have swept across Eastern Europe and the former Soviet Union.

Abraham Lincoln suggested that he saw God's hand similarly operating in the United States in the war between the slave states and free states. A power seems loose in the world, a power that does not condone slavery and repression simply because one group is stronger or richer than another. In South America the movements of oppressed people have been accompanied by new theologies of liberation—theologies that have become as controversial in church hierarchies as in political offices. In our country the civil rights movement was a local expression of this great movement of God. One has only to name these movements to recognize how often the church as an institution has been split and confused by these tides of change. The churches have not often seen these movements —at least in their beginnings—as mission. The church often has been most resistant to these freedom movements. As a matter of fact, the institutional church could sometimes be accused of having colluded with forces that caused the oppression in the first place. And yet thousands of church people have been engaged in these struggles for freedom. In that sense church members have been engaged in this mission. In Eastern Europe the role of the churches was crucial to many of the changes in the social order. As the old order has been overthrown, the churches have been slow to find a role in helping overcome the resulting societal chaos. Traditional mission efforts in many areas, such as Central and West Africa, seem paralyzed by the rapid social changes. How does the institution catch up with God's mission and with its people who are already apostolically engaged? How does the church begin to bring genuine new life to societies and people victorious but confused after casting out one set of demons? In many places the throwing off of colonial oppression has led to other kinds of oppression and subjugation. Without some initiatives that could at least partly come from the churches, we may well find the freed societies to be like the person in the scriptures who was cleansed of one demon only to have it replaced by seven more deadly than the first.

In short, these diverse movements to overthrow oppression seem to bear the mark of something God is doing in our world. That is where the initiative for mission is and always has been. If the church as an institution wants to be engaged in mission, this is a place to connect with what God is doing. Millions of caring people are already engaged in these liberating efforts. The rest of us in the church need to find how we can connect with what God is already about.

The Environmental Movement

A new spirit of stewardship of the earth has emerged in the last few generations. People have responded to that spirit in a myriad of ways. The center of the environmental movement has never been the traditional churches, although people from the churches are found in all the groups concerned for the environment. Many key leaders of the environmental movement are among those I call Christian alumni—people well exposed to the things of faith (early in life or through other people of faith) but no longer "at home" in churches. Current church efforts to establish task forces on environmental issues may be worthwhile but probably will have little impact. The task of the church is to call people and send them into those places in which God's mission is already being done. The church must also articulate and name the mission God is carrying out. In this, as in other areas, the church's task is not to control mission, but to celebrate it, participate in it, and to bring the heritage of faith into the stream of mission.

Human Empowerment

Here I may simply be giving a new "spin" to the first area of God's mission discussed above, freedom movements. But I want to call attention to a new dimension of what God is doing: God is moving to authenticate the specialness of each person and each group. I see many indications of this movement of the Spirit to claim the uniqueness of each person and group and to celebrate it. Equally important is the urgency with which they seek to gain their place at the table of society—the emergence of self-conscious pride among ethnic groups, led in our society by African Americans.[10] The largest, least completed, and most revolutionary empowerment movement has been that of women. This struggle for empowerment is against the structures—many of them church structures or structures in which church systems have colluded—that would deny women their full humanness. God's mission appears to be an affirmation of the integrity and value of every human voice.

Exploring These Areas and the Larger Mission

Churches that want to engage in mission would do well to explore these three areas in which God's mission seems to be running well ahead of our own. My pride in the fact that churches served as training grounds for many of these struggles in no way diminishes my realization of how often the churches have stood against—and still stand against—many areas in which God is engaged in a mission larger than we have on our mission plans and charts!

Within each of these three efforts for human empowerment, there is space and need for those who bear the gospel. All these efforts need the witness of those who bear in their lives the freedom of the gospel and know the ways of demonic powers. These movements, for example, have the potential to ask participants to make the "cause" into an ultimate commitment, sacrificing their own lives for the group. Some of these groups are unrelenting in their pressure on members to turn over their personalities to "the cause." Christians know to be wary of this demon.

I've here discussed three flawed glimpses of what the mission of God today looks like. The mission of God is, of course, much more than these; it is an enormous pressure of loving energy as God reaches out to the world, seeking to touch and heal all its hurts. It is a continuing out-pouring of God's care for the fulfillment of hopes and possibilities, an outpouring that seeks to overcome all forces of enslavement and poverty. The mission of God is connected to God's "heart" and passion for the world and all its inhabitants. The movements of freedom, the new aware-ness of the environment, and the empowerment of human life are but three pulses of that larger concern.

The mission is far greater than our institutional vision of mission has ever imagined. The apostolic church has carved out only a small corner of the mission God has in mind. Mission as interpreted by the church as institution is far too small for the mission of God.

The apostolic task of the people of God is to participate in that larger mission of God. Each person is called to hear and respond to God in the here and now. Each is called to be a servant to humankind and to the world, bringing healing and life, joy and peace. This is not a mission that can be controlled or even authorized by an institution. It is not a mission that awaits the organizational skills of church leaders. It is not a mission to which the church is to deploy its members or for which it is to develop task forces. It is a mission that neither popes nor bishops nor executives nor professors have authority over or even fully understand.

This mission comes to life only as the spread-out people of God reach out to touch whatever is around them—in their jobs, communities, organizations—in their worldly commitments. The mission becomes visible in their actions as servants. Their task: to see that no pain is unshared, no hurt unnoticed, no hunger untouched, no loss grieved alone, no death unknown, and no joy uncelebrated.

Such a people would understand themselves to be apostolic. Their whole life would be sent into God's mission.

What Missional Role Remains for the Institutional Church?

I trust it is clear that the church is not in charge of—has no control over —mission. It needs to move back from thinking that it calls the shots and sets the conditions for mission. It needs to understand mission not in terms of its own aggrandizement or even growth. The mission is God's, and the task of the apostolic people across the globe is to get alongside that mission in their lives.

As for the church, I see four classic patterns for its involvement in God's mission.[11]

Receiving

Institutionally the church is called to open itself to watch and listen for signs of God's mission. This involves keeping the story alive, continuing to hear and study the great works of God in the past so we are better able to recognize God's appearance today. It involves looking with expectation at what the people of God are up to, understanding that the mission of God will be revealed in the pain and joy encountered by people as they live as apostles. It means listening, listening, listening. Listening to what gospel is discovered by the people. Listening to signs of God's mission in the world. Of course this calls the church to move away from its habit of telling and exhorting. Its mode should be receptive. If it is to support an apostolic people, the church must learn to believe what God is and will be doing in God's people. It is to open all the pores of its being to the miracles that God will do through the apostolic, servant people. And it is through this openness that calls will also come to the people.

Offering

Offering is the second mode with which the institution responds to this great mission. I use the term *offering* to mean that the whole experience of the apostolic people is received and becomes that which the church places before God. The offering is celebration and blessing. All the pieces and parts of the world touched by the apostolic people are brought together in prayer and praise. The life of the people becomes the beginning of prayer. As the church takes bread and wine to its altars and holy tables, the church is similarly called to present to God the servant life of its people. In every congregation the gathered people bring with them the worlds they inhabit: the personal—co-workers, neighbors, adversaries, spouses, in-laws; the vocational and institutional—companies, banks, and agencies, universities and offices, white-collar work, blue-collar work, and unemployment. All the realities people live with are received and then made part of the people's conversation with God; they are offered up in celebration.

Identifying

Identification with the pain of the world is the third pattern the church as an institution is to live out. The church as a body receives into itself all the tragedy and pain its people discover in the fallen world in which they serve. The church is to identify itself with the suffering that creeps into every life, every home, every community. The apostolic people bring to the worship of the church all the pain of brokenness they have encountered as they have participated in God's mission of caring for the hurts of the world.

Serving

Finally, the church will release the apostles for service in the world. Having received all that the apostles experienced as servants of the mission, having offered up the life of the world through their experience, having accepted the brokenness and hurt of the world and of change, the church is to release its people for service. It is to release them—not direct them or organize them but release them.

Those patterns are, indeed, liturgical. But they turn liturgy upside down from our usual experience. Instead of bringing stories from scripture to illuminate and direct lives, we need to bring lives to the scripture to discover new visions of our calling. Instead of proclaiming answers, we need a liturgy of openness and expectation. Instead of maintaining a theology of the academy, we need an emerging theology born in the people's engagement with God's mission in the world.

An apostolic people needs a church that supports apostolicity but does not seek to define and control mission. An apostolic people sees its task as that of being servants of humanity and the world. An apostolic people understands mission to be participation in God's mission.

The fifth challenge of the church is to become that apostolic people. This means that every member of the church is called to engage in mission all the time, everywhere.

No small order!

CHAPTER 6

Can These Bones Live?

This book is actually the third in a series. (See "Postlude" at the end of this chapter.) Working on these books, I have had a growing sense of the power and relevance of the biblical images of the Babylonian exile. My question "Do we have time?" is a pale version of Ezekiel's question to God as Ezekiel stood before a graphic vision of a valley heaped with dry bones. He asked, "Can these bones live?" Let us review the historical context of that question.

The history of the people of Israel is an unprecedented and still un-surpassed story in world history. A little more than three thousand years ago, a small band of slaves somehow escaped servitude in Egypt; they preserved their memories of that moment as a point of deliverance by God—the story of the parting and crossing of the Red Sea. Whatever that story meant (the movie version with waves standing rigid as walls or the more liberal version of high winds sweeping water away from a swampy area[1]), within a few generations that small band of slaves began to turn the world upside down. They may have embellished their story, but they nevertheless took some incredible steps.

They conceived a moral code grounded in their experience of God—the Ten Commandments, a code that has not yet been surpassed. Beginning with the Red Sea story, they conceived of a God who had purpose and direction. In short, they began to invent history. All this, remember, beginning from incredibly modest beginnings, as slaves.

This band of outsiders gradually built the strength and unity with which to claim and settle some of the most disputed land in the world—the western end of the Fertile Crescent, at the crossroads of the then-known world. They overthrew the inhabitants of the land.[2] A chaotic period followed during which this new nation faced constant challenges by people passing through the area or trying to supplant them. With no political system beyond their tribal alliances, they discovered how to meet crises—by raising up heroic figures they called judges who rallied the people against their many enemies with mixed success. The need for a more dependable political structure led them to invent a monarchy.

Two of the greatest kings of the ancient world—David and Solomon—came to the throne. Under David the people overpowered the fortress of Jerusalem—Zion—and immediately started to see it as the Holy City. Solomon's building of the temple—one of the wonders of the world—was not as wonderful as what the temple embodied: the development of a comprehensive theology growing from the early experiences, crossing the Red Sea and wandering in the wilderness. The temple became a holy place, replacing the portable Ark of the Covenant; it was there in the temple that the people's dialogue with God occurred.

Remember, this all started at what to us looks like ground zero. In some three to four hundred years, these incredible moral, theological, and political inventions were made by these people—moved by their God. In all of human history I do not know of a people who came so far so fast. Of course there were problems, but even the problems were celebrated in poetry and writings that, in themselves, were unprecedented for their variety and literary quality.

During the next generations, things seemed to fall apart. Division crept in. Civil war led to a split kingdom, two monarchies. Unjust kings reigned. The people and their leaders regularly fell away from the vision of earlier years. One of the two kingdoms was overcome by a foreign power.

But even those setbacks generated new reflection on God's purposes, a new deepening of a consciousness of a moral order. Extraordinary prophets emerged from the life of the people, holding up a plumb line to call the people back to God's ways. The tradition and writing of the prophets added a richness again unparalleled in the ancient world. Out of their failures, the Hebrews produced the work of Jeremiah and Amos.

And all through these lean years, the people grew more strongly attached to the meaning of Jerusalem and the temple. These realities stood for the special call of the people before God. They became the embodiment of the story.

And this incredible story was the background for Ezekiel's question, "Can these bones live?" In 587 B.C.E. the story of this remarkable people came to an end—so far as they could see. Nebuchadnezzar's armies conquered Jerusalem, the Holy City, and leveled the temple—the place through which their contact with God was mediated. The *only* place, they thought hopelessly. The temple vessels were even taken away to grace the altars of foreign gods in Babylon. Leaders of the nation were led away in chains to an exile far from their beloved city.

When in history has such a story been told? When has such incredible vitality and imagination, sheer inventiveness, made such a civilization in just a few centuries, then to be completely destroyed, as if forever? We can understand the people's shock, dismay, loss of hope. Exiled from the center of their life. Exiled, it seemed, even from their God. Rejected by God.

Exiled Ezekiel asked a question that was about more than whether they could ever return to Jerusalem. It included a prophetic statement that the people had fallen away from the relationship that had given them life. They had become not only exiles, but also dead and dry to their vocation to be God's people.

The situation was hopeless. No way was open.

That is precisely why I call on Ezekiel's question for us today in the churches. In spite of the fact that we are surrounded by great church buildings, theologies, and traditions, I believe the life has disappeared from many of the structures that have been so important and supportive for us. As the people of Israel were separated from the traditions that had given them life, so more and more of us in the churches are finding ourselves separated from that which gave life to previous generations. I sometimes think the people of Israel were in one way more fortunate than we are; they were physically uprooted and separated from their Jerusalem; they had no way to disguise those hard realities. They woke up every morning and saw Babylon, not Jerusalem, outside their windows.

We still wake up in the morning thinking we are in Jerusalem. Until a generation or so ago that *seemed* to be true. But now we wake up finding ourselves in Babylon. *We* can fool ourselves in ways they could not. We look out the window and see all the furniture of our supposed Jerusalem: churches on the corners, some of them bursting at the seams. And yet more and more of us have begun to realize that the world we inhabit is not Jerusalem. We live in Babylon. And I see no signs that Babylon is going to become Jerusalem.

How can we sing the Lord's song in this foreign land? Can these bones live? Is there time?

I take hope from what happened to the people of Israel while they were in exile. Consider the seventy years of the exile. (It is no accident when I say that I look forward to at least three generations of difficult times for us in the churches.) What did the people do in those years of exile? Having lost all the supports for their faith and community, what did they do? I see four critical answers to that question.[3]

First, they wrote the Bible. Of course that is an exaggeration. They had many pieces already written. Stories. Poems. Bits and pieces. But while they were in Babylon (not Jerusalem) the segments were stitched together, and important new pieces were written. Far from home, they set about the task of remembering who they were. My personal hunch is that they fully understood the miracle at the Red Sea only after they were exiled, far from home. And in Babylon they wrote the story, answering "Who are we and to what are we called?"

What's more, they realized they needed to study the story, to reflect on its meanings. They invented a place where they could gather for study, the synagogue.

Similarly, they invented the role of the teacher. From that time on, the religious leadership of the rabbi was a central ingredient in the growth of the people's consciousness.

Perhaps most important, the people discovered how the faith did not depend upon the temple; it could be carried from generation to generation through the teaching and witness of the family. Modes of celebration of the great events of the history of the people were developed from home liturgy and celebration.

By the end of the exile, the Jewish people had put together the essential tools they needed for survival. Those essentials served them well for 2,500 years, holding them steady and maintaining their identity as a people and sense of vocation in dispersion all across the globe. Even if they had never returned to Jerusalem—and many never did—they had the resources to live in dispersion.

By the power of God, the bones did come to life.

There is good news for us in this story. Not easy news, but good news.

I do not believe we face greater challenges than did the exiles in Babylon. Our challenge is to change the ownership of the church and involves freeing ourselves from some of the unproductive power issues. We need to find a way for the laity and the clergy to enter into creative dialogue for the growth of the body. Remember, God helped the people in Babylon to begin to define the nature of the rabbinate.

Our second challenge is to find more appropriate and workable structures for the life of faith. (In Babylon a people who had lost the locus of their life of worship discovered the life of the synagogue.)

Our third challenge is to find a way to express a fuller spirituality in dependence on the Spirit of God. What else did the people of Israel do but learn that the Spirit of God was not limited to the structure of the temple? The Spirit went with them, bringing life wherever they were called to go.

Our fourth challenge is to find community with one another and to find how to share that in our world. (The end product of the Babylonian exile was a people with a clear sense of identity and an ability to make that identity portable.)

Our fifth challenge is to become an apostolic people. (Since the exile, the people of Israel have known themselves to be marked by God, and they bear that mark, even among aliens and into persecution, because they claim that identity.)

I must state one important caveat. The great creative adaptation of the people of Israel began when they discovered that they were living in Babylon. I believe we in the churches are, indeed, in a foreign land, our own Babylon. But too many of us continue to pretend that we are surrounded by the comfortable walls of Jerusalem, safe in the shadow of the temple. Or we think we have only to make a few adjustments to the city wall or the architecture of the temple to return to the comfortable days we think we had in the past.

No. The bones really are dry.

But I have enormous confidence in the One who led the people through the Red Sea to become a great people. I have great confidence in the One who went into exile with the people and led them to new life there, bringing dry bones to life. I have even greater confidence in the One who lived among us as our servant, died, and was raised to new life to open that life to us. And in these later days, when we seem to have strayed away from what Christ calls us to, I have confidence that he continues to call and that he will shape our life to reflect his loving will for us and for all humankind.

What will the future hold for the church? Who can know? What would you have said the future held for the band of shackled captives being driven down the road to Babylon?

What we can know is that God is faithful. We can know that in Babylon God called a lost people, and they responded. Their bones were covered with sinew and flesh and then brought to life by the breath of God. We can trust that God will be faithful to us through our times of change and trial. When, in God's providence, these dry bones leap to life, we will discover again the powerful breath of the Spirit, bringing us and the church of the future to new life.

Author's Note

This is the third book of a series I did not know I was writing as a series.[1] The books have grown out of a forty-year dialogue I have had with people in churches. The books all come out of my conviction that the way we have "done church" over the past few generations has stopped working.

The first book, *The Once and Future Church,* came out of my observations of church life and my teaching about church tensions. I was teaching some of the material a decade before I wrote it down. But during long-range strategic planning that preceded my retirement from the presidency of The Alban Institute, I was given an assignment by consultants Vance and Mary Sharer Johnson. "Your job," they told me, "is to articulate the vision that has driven this institute." I did the best I could to come up with the classic "twenty-five words or less" vision statement, but I simply could not do it. So I sat down and wrote it as a series of articles that laid out what I saw happening in the churches and how my colleagues and I at The Alban Institute were attempting to respond. It eventually became that first book.

Anyone working with congregations today knows the sheer hard work required of church leaders, lay or clergy. Anyone knows that things that worked well a generation ago no longer work. Anyone knows that the local structures get out of alignment with the regional or national church structures. I observed that whatever was going wrong was generating a massive amount of anger and scapegoating. People at all levels were trying to "blame" somebody else for the pain they were experiencing.

The book was an attempt to point out that the dislocations were objective changes that were also occuring in the larger society. I believed and wanted to stress that there was no plot afoot; we happened to be living in a time of changing understandings. In terms of the modern jargon, the paradigms were shifting.

That first book offered no solutions but provided a perspective to allow us to see where we are and stop blaming each other. Apparently the book worked for many people. It gave names to some causes of pain. Though I am no historian, I received requests to teach about shifts of history.[2] The Evangelical Lutheran Church in Canada hired me to be keynoter of their conference on the subject, a conference they daringly named Holy Shift.[3]

Questions people asked pushed me to think about some of the next steps. If I could not tell what we must do to change the church that "wasn't working," could I at least try to state what kind of church we might need in the future? As I worked with and learned from others and as I reviewed the work of the past generation or two of pioneers in church change, I saw sets of functions that have marked the life of the church in all previous generations.

The second book of the series, *Transforming Congregations for the Future,* came out of that effort to describe the key functions we need to include in the life of the church in any generation. If we understood how we got to be in the fix we are in—and *The Once and Future Church* tried to provide clarity on that point—I hoped we could initiate changes as we identified some of the functions we needed to reconstitute for tomorrow's church. To survive, the church must provide answers for some very pragmatic needs. In denomination after denomination I saw cutbacks being done in a haphazard way simply to make a budget balance. Considering budget restraints and societal pressures, we needed to make changes consciously—not haphazardly—in a way that would preserve vital dimensions of the church.[4]

As I continued working with people in different denominations, they asked me what we needed to do to build the church of the future. I remain very skittish in making prescriptions because I feel that the church will include many churches, many shapes of religious institutional life. I believe the church will grow organically out of the diversity and richness of the churches we have today.

In March 1995, Dr. Francis Wade, rector of my parish, Saint Alban's Episcopal in Washington, D.C., asked me to breakfast and gave me a commission: "Would you put together your ideas about what the church must face in the next generation or two to rebuild its life for the future?" He elaborated, "What challenges do we face? What roadblocks must we get around?" He then asked me to present those ideas in a Sunday sermon.

I gave the sermon and kept working on the idea. In the year since then I have worked and reworked to try to be clearer and more helpful to those who are trying to work for that church of tomorrow. I have shared these ideas with a number of audiences, with the Urban-Suburban Clergy Group of the Episcopal Church, with Hillside Christian Church, with two groups in continuing education programs at the Toronto School of Theology, and as a set of lectures for the religion department of the Chautauqua Institution in New York. Every time I have shared the ideas I have learned from those who have reacted to them. In this final shape— here in this book—they are deeply influenced by scores of people who have asked me questions, who have argued with me, and many who have shown me the error of my ways. I am grateful to them all. Where I am able to identify the contributions of others I try to give credit, but I am aware that almost everything I know and believe has been given me by this community of faith in which I work.

That community and that conversation continue to exist. I expect and welcome comments from friends and critics. That is an open invitation to you in two ways: First, take these ideas and generate your own in your life and work. Go beyond what I think and know. Second, if you feel the urge, write me to add to or to challenge my understanding and knowledge.

The most important message from me is this: Your congregation is where you touch this worldwide set of challenges. Engage them there. Give it your best. And tell us how it goes. Help build a life-giving community of faith for tomorrow.

Introduction

1. I have frequently argued the equally false opposite of this statement—that churches are not entirely different from other organizations. Both are true. In many ways they do interact quite similarly to businesses, schools, etc. The problem is in overidentification or overdifferentiation.

2. John P. Kotter, "Why Transformation Efforts Fail," *Harvard Business Review*, March-April 1995, 59ff.

3. A friend gave me an unelegant image of this: "Some people think you can replicate a mocking bird's song if you stuff enough mockingbirds in a sausage machine. You don't get a song. You get an inedible, useless mess."

4. Kotter's eight points are all useful, but the three I have presented seem most directly applicable to the churches.

Chapter 1

1. "Isms" are the way most of us get in touch with what Paul calls "powers and principalities" (Eph. 6:12). They are demonic powers larger than the individual, and they influence and shape us in ways we are usually not aware of. Christians can recognize the power of these influences and realize that just to name them is to gain some power over them. We also must acknowledge that even these powers are subject to the One in whom we live and move. Indeed, knowing all this allows Christians to know that we *are* racist and clericalist and sexist—but that we are working to recover! And we are praying for the overthrow of the demonic powers. Our hearts are attractive targets for the demons' powers. We do well to maintain our vigilance and our humility in the face of them.

2. I first tried this fable out on my friend and mentor Verna Dozier—to try to articulate why it seems so hard to change from the clericalism that characterizes the church both of us know and love.

3. See Dean Hoge, Jackson W. Carroll, and Francis K. Scheets, *Patterns of Parish Leadership* (Kansas City, MO: Sheed & Ward, 1988).

4. The research by Hoge, Carroll, and Scheets (ibid.) was done in four denominations. In all of those denominations it was clear how normative this standard has become for the laity. When asked what form of leadership lay leaders needed in their congregations, the answer was overwhelmingly "fully trained, full-time clergy." The answer was the same regardless of the possibility or impossibility of funding such leadership.

5. I remember a classic illustration from my work with churches in New Zealand. The indigenous Maori people in the churches had denominational differences described in terms of the difference between the Greek words *homoousious* and *homoiousious*.

6. I am aware that this is a controversial comment backed only by my observation. The only empirical evidence I have seen was compiled in the early seventies by a consultant to Intermet Seminary who tried to determine how administrators at theological seminaries made decisions about their institutions. He found no instance of basic seminary planning in which administrators applied any theological concepts or criteria to the program options. Decisions were based on budget and political influence.

7. Parker Palmer, speaking of the experience of a small group of Quakers in the eastern U.S., suggests that their ability to change the pattern resulted from a decision not to eliminate the clergy, but to eliminate the laity.

8. The simplest statement is the brief piece, Bruce Reed and Barry Palmer, *The Task of the Church and the Role of Its Members* (Bethesda, MD: The Alban Institute, 1975). Reed's fuller treatment of these issues, published in the late seventies, is now out of print: *The Dynamics of Religion* (London: Darton, Longman, and Todd).

9. Edwin A. Friedman, *From Generation to Generation: Family Process in Church and Synagogue* (New York: Guilford Press, 1985).

10. I note particularly for its accessibility Peter Steinke, *How Your Church Family Works* (Bethesda, MD: The Alban Institute, 1993).

11. The Alban Institute published a number of pieces about the interim pastorate. It also helped launch the Interim Pastor Network, which

meets annually and continues to train interim pastors. Several denominations have their own groups of interim pastors. My own statements about that ministry are found in Loren Mead, *Critical Moment of Ministry: A Change of Pastors* (Bethesda, MD: The Alban Institute, 1986).

Chapter 2

1. Loren Mead, *The Once and Future Church* (Bethesda, MD: The Alban Institute, 1991).

2. Loren Mead, *Transforming Congregations for the Future* (Bethesda, MD: The Alban Institute, 1994).

3. I am personally aware of many regional judicatories that sponsor "resource centers" to help congregations get better access to educational and program resources. Very few of these are much more than a gloomy closet in an office building, containing poorly cataloged educational material stuffed onto poorly lit shelves. This continuation of duplicative, inadequate denominational effort comes in spite of a few brilliant examples of resource centers that specialize in delivering help. I think especially of the group of Parish Resource Centers created by Douglas Whiting in Lancaster, Pennsylvania, and now including similar centers on Long Island, in Dayton, Denver, and South Bend. Judicatories also wastefully duplicate the use of outside resources. At The Alban Institute we often found that three different consultants had been contracted to lead an educational event, such as conflict management, within a fifty-mile radius in a period of two months. Waste!

4. See Mead, *Transforming Congregations for the Future,* ch. 4.

5. I am aware of the work, now well over a decade old, being done in Nevada by Episcopalians. Other pioneering has begun in the Episcopal Diocese of Northern Michigan.

6. See Robert Wuthnow, *The Restructuring of American Religion* (Princeton, NJ: Princeton University Press, 1988). In this fine book Wuthnow makes a case that the political conservatives of many denominations and the political liberals of those same denominations may be moving toward functional coalitions despite the denominational differences.

7. Those *do* remain substantial differences, one invisible, the other visible. The *visible* difference is between those who view the scriptures as inerrant and understand faith by "fundamentals" and those who do not. The invisible difference is the cultural difference between premillennialists and postmillennialists. What I am talking about as the diminished

difference between the denominations is especially true of the "mainline" denominations, but not restricted to them.

8. See Mead, *The Once and Future Church.*

9. This illustration comes from work of the Institute for Christian and Jewish Studies, a remarkable coalition in Baltimore. In Washington, DC, the Interfaith Council annually hosts an interfaith celebration in a great concert of music from seven faiths.

Chapter 3

1. Parker Palmer, Tilden Edwards, and James Simmons—all later better known for teaching and writing. Tilden is the founder of the Shalem Institute for Spiritual Formation in Washington, DC.

2. Jean Haldane, *Religious Pilgrimages* (Bethesda, MD: The Alban Institute, 1975).

3. Paul clearly recognizes the practice of *glossalia* as fairly widespread in the early church. In contrast to a literal reading of Acts 2, in which speaking in tongues is taken to mean speaking in the languages of different nationalities, *glossalia* is ecstatic utterance, often within worship.

4. Harvey Cox, *Fire from Heaven* (Reading, MA: Addison-Wesley, 1995). A fascinating and sweeping story of Pentecostalism and the charismatic movement in the twentieth century.

5. There is some cultural chauvinism in this remark. Since beginning this chapter, I have become aware of strong "charismatic" outbreaks in many other parts of the world in this and in earlier centuries.

6. I do not say this very clearly because it is too close for comfort. Being aware of a pressure from Someone beyond myself, I have found myself called to *do* something that breaks all the rules. Such impulses are not always from the Spirit, I ruefully note, but there have been moments when my impulse *was* from the Spirit and lives changed as a result. For *me,* those moments have tended to be in situations of community, often in worship.

7. Barry Johnson, *Polarity Management: Identifying and Managing Unsolvable Problems* (Amherst, MA: HRD Press, 1992).

8. Corrine Ware, *Discover Your Spiritual Type* (Bethesda, MD: The Alban Institute, 1995), has provided us with a new framework for understanding spirituality in a wholistic way. She gives a model for understanding the relationship of different kinds of spirituality, and she also

provides tools for people and congregations wanting to explore the full dimensions of spirituality. I am particularly grateful to her for building in the idea of the late U. T. Holmes, Jr., whose tragic loss in 1981 still hurts.

See also Donald Hands and Wayne Fehr, *Spiritual Wholeness for Clergy* (Bethesda, MD: The Alban Institute, 1993). They explore a wholistic approach to spirituality, starting with clinical studies of clergy who had burned out spiritually. The learnings of this study of clergy spirituality have much to teach about building healthier, more comprehensive models of spirituality.

Chapter 4

1. John W. Gardner, *Building Community* (Washington, DC: Independent Sector, 1991), 5. Used by permission.

2. Gibson Winter captured the meaning of this migration for American churches in his analysis, *The Suburban Captivity of the Churches* (Garden City, NY: Doubleday, 1961).

3. See Samuel Freedman, *Upon This Rock: The Miracles of a Black Church* (San Francisco: HarperCollins, 1993), the story of a great African-American congregation in Brooklyn.

4. *The Downsizing of America: Millions of Americans Are Losing Good Jobs. This Is Their Story* (New York: Random House, 1996). This book is a compilation of articles printed in the *New York Times*.

5. "For an AT&T Brat, the Anguish of Letting Go," *New York Times*, 14 January 1996, 12.

6. One can see the frightening reality of such communities when they go to war with one another, as they do regularly at European soccer matches!

7. "Owners' New Strategy: Take the Team and Run," *New York Times,* 14 January 1996, sec. 8, p. 1.

8. Robert D. Putnam, "Bowling Alone: America's Declining Social Capital," *Journal of Democracy* 6, no. 1 (January 1995), 65-77.

9. Ibid., 70. Putnam indicates the size of the phenomenon he's talking about: "nearly 80 million Americans went bowling at least once in 1993, nearly a third more than voted in the 1994 Congressional elections."

10. In fact, his basic contention is refuted sharply by Robert J. Samuelson in an op-ed column, "'Bowling Alone' Is Bunk," *Washington Post,* 10 April 1996. Samuelson marshals impressive data of his own while questioning a number of Putnam's conclusions. What may be the

most fascinating element in this exchange is the way the Putnam thesis seems to have touched something the public recognized as a felt reality. My hunch is that people will remember "Bowling Alone" a lot longer than "'Bowling Alone' Is Bunk" because the former seems to explain something Americans both fear and sense to be happening to them and around them. The fear and anxiety may be more "real" than the statistics.

11. William Raspberry, "Crisis of Community," *Sewanee*, January 1996.

12. Robert Bellah, et al., *Habits of the Heart* (Berkeley: University of California Press, 1985).

13. Garrett Hardin, in a provocatively simple paper now nearly three decades old, points to a basic problem we have in seeking the experience of community. In "The Tragedy of the Commons," *Science* (1968), Hardin suggests that our society is constructed by assumptions in which individual self-interest is in conflict with being in community. He argues that genuine "community" has to be based in a larger view of life than simple self-interest. The strengths of his article are its simple statement of profound truth (analogous to Putnam's article on bowling) and its basis in economic analysis—a dimension often overlooked by those who try to engineer society to provide community.

14. Britton Johnston and Sally Johnson, *Saints and Neighbors* (Chicago: Center for Church and Community Ministries at McCormick Seminary, 1991). The project from which these stories come was productive in other ways: Carl Dudley, director of the project, wrote two other books on the experience—*Basic Steps to Community Ministry* (Bethesda, MD: The Alban Institute, 1991) and the more recent *Next Steps in Community Ministry* (Bethesda, MD: The Alban Institute, 1996).

15. John E. Linnan, as quoted in *National Catholic Reporter,* 31 May 1996, 6. Linnan is a teacher at the Catholic Theological Union in Chicago.

16. *Research Project: Attitudes and Perceptions about the Church.* The study was done for the United Methodist Church, Kansas West Conference, 1994.

17. Reginald Bibby, *There's Got to Be More* (Winfield, BC, Canada: Wood Lake Books, 1995).

18. Dean Hoge, Benton Johnson, and Donald Luidens, *Vanishing Boundaries* (Louisville: Westminster/John Knox, 1994). See especially 132-144.

19. See Charles Olsen, *Transforming Church Boards* (Bethesda, MD: The Alban Institute, 1995). Olsen has been following the issue of church as community for years. I first knew him through his 1970s research on house churches in Project Base Church. His new book comes from the conviction that congregations will not become spiritual communities until church boards themselves become spiritual communities. The book details his research on the subject but also gives practical help to those who want to help their church boards in this critical transformation.

20. It is tragic that many churches are having such a struggle separating out "valid" from "invalid" forms of human family—with distinctions based on sexual behavior. Clearly the function I am describing here requires the churches to support human community wherever it is exercised to the spiritual and personal growth of persons. The affirmation of community is essential; the form of it may be argued.

21. Research by the Independent Sector and others indicates that people who belong to churches and religious congregations are much more likely than nonmembers to be volunteers and donors to community causes.

22. Although I do have difficulty when a denomination denounces Walt Disney and others boycott Proctor and Gamble for alleged cultural sell-outs.

23. C. Ellis Nelson, beloved wise man of Christian education in the Presbyterian Church, puts it bluntly: "Let's face it, friends. Sunday school will no longer cut it!" Unpublished quote from an address to Presbyterian educators and pastors, 1996.

24. One of the first books published by The Alban Institute was titled *A Way to Belong*. In that book, Celia Allison Hahn explored the very special way one congregation—Saint Mark's Episcopal Church in Washington, D.C.—designed and carried out a way for new members to learn the values and meanings of congregational belonging. The thesis was that all congregations need to be clear about designing a way to belong. The book is out of print.

25. Although I have tried to practice tithing for many years, I still have a lot of questions about it. I'm worried about the legalistic way it is often used and also about the crazy theological ideas that sometimes seem to grow up like weeds around it.

Chapter 5

1. The best overall study of the development of consciousness of
mission is David Bosch, *Transforming Mission* (Maryknoll, NY: Orbis,
1991). A provocative counterpoint to the internal tensions in the church
regarding the meaning of outreach to the Jews is found in Elaine Pagel,
The Origin of Satan (New York: Random House, 1995).

2. Matthew 28:18-20. A strength of Bosch's *Transforming Mission*
is his careful study of biblical sources; he indicates there were a variety
of understandings of *mission*. Our inherited understanding of the biblical
record comes from focusing for centuries on this one Matthew theme,
which won the day.

3. I realize that thousands of people engaged in the face-to-face
work of mission went far beyond the stereotypes and came to a deep
appreciation of the uniqueness of the cultures and people they encountered. I am speaking of the popular sense of that mission and much of the
motivation for engaging in it.

4. Frankly, it seems as if a lot of the discussions of church union
today take their point of departure from those relatively fruitless discussions.

5. See D. Hoge, B. Johnson, and D. Luidens, *Vanishing Boundaries*
(Louisville: Westminster/John Knox Press, 1994). These authors describe churched populations as having about as much "trickled down"
theological knowledge as those who are totally unchurched.

6. I am deeply indebted to the work of Robert J. Schreiter, *Constructing Local Theologies* (Maryknoll, NY: Orbis, 1993). Schreiter
breaks new ground in the theology and strategy of mission. This book
and Bosch's *Transforming Mission* have the potential to blow out of the
water much of our mission practice and offer a beginning place for a
genuinely comprehensive picture of the mission of the future. These are
very significant books.

7. I am deeply indebted in this section to the work of Schreiter,
Constructing Local Theologies, and Bosch, *Transforming Mission.*

8. Schreiter, *Constructing Local Theologies,* points to the critical but
limited role of the church in this larger mission of God, saying first that
"the development of local theologies depends as much on finding Christ
already active in the culture as it does on bringing Christ to the culture"
(p. 29). But he goes on to say, "for a local theology to become a Christian local theology, it must have a genuine encounter with the Christian

tradition" (p. 34). Between these two sentences hangs the dilemma of how any of us with faith communicate it to those who have not yet found it.

9. As I name and briefly describe these movements of the mission of God, I am very aware that I see only what I see and that final judgment on these movements will not be in for generations. "By their fruits you shall know them."

10. Consider the impact of Stokely Carmichael's cry, "Black Power," which transformed a struggle about civil rights into a crusade for racial and personal pride in identity.

11. In my book *Transforming Congregations for the Future*, I discuss another four—the four functions congregations need to carry out as they equip people to become apostolic. Those four are programmatic functions: the tasks of (1) proclamation, (2) teaching, (3) serving, and (4) building community. Here I am pointing to the church's spiritual involvement in God's mission. Old friends will detect the influence of Dom Gregory Dix.

Chapter 6

1. I can live with almost any interpretation, but I do find it difficult to sing the hymn line that refers to walking through the Red Sea with "unmoistened foot." I sense it must at least have been muddy.

2. Modern biblical scholarship suggests that the story we have received exaggerates the unity and cohesion of the people in the beginning, and that numbers of people and tribes gradually were brought into the identity of the Hebrew people. If this is true, this is an even greater miracle than the biblical story.

3. In these four points I am greatly oversimplifying. Most of these elements have a more complex history, but critical, if not formative, parts took place in these years of exile.

Postlude

1. Loren Mead, *The Once and Future Church* (Bethesda, MD: The Alban Institute, 1991); *Transforming Congregations for the Future* (Bethesda, MD: The Alban Institute, 1994).

2. See also David Bosch, *Transforming Mission* (Maryknoll, NY: Orbis Books, 1991). I continually refer people to this as an excellent introduction to the real history I skim over in my book.

3. Complete with t-shirts emblazoned with "Holy Shift" on the front and "Shift Happens" on the back.

4. Some people have found my book *More Than Numbers* (Bethesda, MD: The Alban Institute, 1993) to be a very practical help in their work in congregations. I have to admit that I wrote *More Than Numbers* before I had any plan to write *Transforming Congregations*. *More Than Numbers* was an effort to make available some of the practical tools I had found useful in working with congregations. It was not intended to be part of this series that I did not yet know I was writing. Several other books of mine are similarly unrelated and deal with other church issues.